THE BOMBAY PALACE COOKBOOK

THE
BOMBAY PALACE
COOKBOOK

A Treasury of Indian Delights

STENDAHL

CARAVAN PUBLISHING,   NEW YORK

Dedicated to the men of the Bombay Palace kitchens,
whose skills have made
a complex cuisine
seem simple.

A CARAVAN PUBLISHING GROUP BOOK

Published by Caravan Publishing, N.Y.

Manufactured in Italy.
Designed by Laura Hough.

First Edition

Library of Congress Cataloging in Publication Data

Stendahl.
  The Bombay Palace cookbook.

  Includes index.
  1. Cookery, Indic. I. Bombay Palace (Firm)
II. Title.
TX724.5.I4S74   1985   641.5954   84-28654
ISBN 0-396-08577-6

Contents

LIST OF COLOR PLATES

Preface

In a land whose population is second only to China's, and where there are fourteen major languages and over two hundred fifty dialects, cooking as well as everything else is a complex affair. Since Indian cooking has traditionally been done over small charcoal fires and with only basic utensils, Indian cooks became painstaking detailists—quite appropriate to a land where time is cheap.

A chief value of this book is that its recipes, while both authentic and classical in nature, have been streamlined to better suit Americans who cannot afford to spend too much time preparing meals.

A successful restaurant must turn out many different dishes in a short space of time. Thus certain time-saving techniques must be developed to shorten cooking chores without sacrificing quality. The highly efficient shortcuts perfected in the Bombay Palace kitchens have been incorporated into the recipes of this book. They will make you a fine Indian cook without excessive demands on your time.

In addition, we have included two "master demonstration recipes" that explain in step-by-step detail some of the basics that shape modern, efficient Indian cooking. If you master the techniques outlined in these mini cooking lessons, you will soon have the skills and confidence to create your very own variations from scratch.

Good luck and good cooking!

Chapter 1

THE MAN WHO BUILT
THE PALACE

Set in Rockefeller Center, New York City's Bombay Palace is the flagship of a growing fleet of low-keyed, elegant dining establishments. Through its doors come diplomats and dignitaries, media stars and politicians . . . the rich and famous and the not-so-famous . . . all of them intent on sampling the delicacies of the justly famous Punjab cuisine. With eight restaurants now in operation and a dozen more in the planning, the Bombay Palace fleet is the largest array of Indian restaurants in the world. Sant Chatwal planned it that way. He's the man who built the Palace.

When I think of Sant Singh Chatwal I tend to imagine him standing in the middle of the dining room of one of his restaurants, arms folded, surveying the scene. Handsome, dark-eyed and bearded, he wears a black suit and a distinctive crimson turban, looking very much like a Punjabi nobleman. "I feel rather like an ambassador," he is apt to smile, "bringing my native foods and culture to the people of the world."

Chatwal grew up in the Punjab, a region of Northern India known for its elaborate cuisine and its earthy, colorful people who love to eat and drink. The son of a merchant, the young Chatwal loved travelling with his father on business, listening and learning as he talked with people of every sort. Always he wanted to do something adventurous; so by the time he was twenty he was a fighter pilot in the Indian Air Force.

Chatwal has a restless soul. After a few years, even flying became boring; so he headed for Ethiopia, dreaming of doing something different. In Addis Ababa he discovered an interesting Middle Eastern restaurant called the Omar Khayyam, and he began going there every day for lunch and dinner. The place became his home away from home. After a year and a half, the owner—who was by now Chatwal's close friend—went to London on business for a couple of months, leaving his restaurant in Chatwal's care.

The two months turned into a year, and Chatwal became first a partner and then owner of the restaurant, working sixteen-hour days, getting a crash course in the restaurant business. From the staff he learned about service; in the kitchen he studied the chefs at work; in the dining room he talked with the customers.

"What I really enjoyed most was talking with people," Chatwal recalls. "I said to myself, here I am in Ethiopia meeting Americans, Canadians, Europeans and Indians, serving them unusual foods that they all like. I must open a place of my own—an Indian restaurant!"

He returned home to India to research the idea. Visiting the best restaurants and hotel chains, he sought out the foremost chefs. By offering them better wages and a chance to be creative, he convinced them to come with him. Allowing his cooks the freedom to be inventive is part of Chatwal's genius. As a result, his people have developed and created a number of Indian dishes that are not duplicated in any other restaurants.

Blending native tastes and the unique spices and sauces of his Northern India, Chatwal tailored his own kind of menu, one he thought would please the palates of the widely divergent types of people he wished to serve. His approach met with gratifying success. Within eight years the young entrepreneur (he's still under forty) has opened restaurants in London, Paris, New York, Chicago, Los Angeles, Washington, D.C., Houston, Vancouver, Toronto and Montreal.

Keys to Chatwal's success have been consistency and good taste. In his establishments dishes are done according to the classical Indian manner, but they have a subtle individual stamp: "Even when I open a restaurant in India it will be something different," Chatwal insists. "You won't find dishes exactly like ours in any Indian restaurant—anywhere."

A cuisine of great delicacy and imagination, the Punjabi recipes are centuries old, originating in the royal kitchens of the Moghuls, the ancient rulers of Northern India. To those ancient recipes, Chatwal's chefs have added a modern flavor, refining them to suit the Western palate. While Chatwal's greatest challenge has been to educate people to appreciate true Indian cuisine, he demands perfection from his chefs, and his Palaces have consistently been awarded top ratings by food critics.

As he travels about the world checking on his restaurants, Sant Chatwal reflects on where his next adventure will be. He says he is a happy man. "I'm constantly learning new things . . . there's always something different happening in my life. But what is most exciting is that I'm doing what nobody has ever tried to do before—taking Indian cuisine around the world!"

Chapter 2

THE INDIAN KITCHEN

The Moghlai Cuisine

In the Northern part of India lies the Punjab, a beautiful and fertile area, where the cuisine of the Moghuls originated. The Moghlai cuisine is considered the richest, most lavish and subtlest of all the regional styles of Indian cookery. Centuries ago this cuisine was enriched by the conquering Persians who were then at the height of their civilization. Meat eaters and wheat eaters, the Punjabi consume little rice, the mainstay of most Indians, although they have since adopted and adapted the finest vegetarian recipes of the Hindus and other non-meat-eating religious sects.

In the Moghlai tradition, food is intricately and subtly spiced; Moghlai cookery is famous for its delicate seasonings, full-flavored spices gently used, for its creamy yoghurt-based marinades, and for the use of nut meats to add a lavish touch to a meat or rice dish. Complex, elusive tastes are more desirable than spicy hotness. Ghee is the cooking fat used rather than the vegetable oils of other parts of the subcontient. Ghee (see p. 11) is clarified butter, useful because it keeps for a long time and does not smoke during the cooking process.

Basmati rice is used in the colorful and extravagant rice and vegetable or rice and meat dishes, usually called biryanis, pillaws or pulaos. Basmati rice is unsurpassed for flavor and texture by any other rice in the world (see pp. 10, 150). There

4

is a saying, "When you smell the beautiful fragrance of basmati rice cooking, you know your neighbor is having special guests."

The special charcoal cooking of the tandoor (see p. 110) is also a feature of Moghlai cuisine.

The Bombay Palace menu, upon which most of this book is based, features many superb examples of Moghlai cooking. However, exciting recipes from other cuisines are also found both on the menu and in our book. While there are real differences in the food styles of the vast Indian subcontinent, through the centuries exchanges and variations have taken place that tend to blend the distinctions. Thus, here you will find not only the fundamentals of the Moghlai cuisine but also examples of vegetarian cooking, fish cookery, meat cookery and even recipes using pork from the Portuguese-influenced port of Goa.

Moghlai cooking is basically very healthful. Curries had been eaten for centuries before anyone considered the fact that the spices used in Indian cooking were rich in vitamins and other nutrients. In ancient days, food preparation was akin to a religious ritual, and many dishes were put together with the calculated aim of introducing medicinal herbs and spices into the diet.

Indian cooking makes extensive use of chilies, and the *Capsicum* family has been acknowledged by modern nutritionists to be a richer source of vitamin C than citrus fruits. Lime and lemon juice, also used frequently, are of course also good sources of this vitamin.

Ginger has for centuries been used by both Indians and the Chinese as a medicine, and is mentioned in both Sanskrit literature and the Talmud.

Both garlic and onions are among our most health-sustaining vegetables. In many lands, folk medicine has recommended smelling onions and eating the bulb itself as a cure for colds. Some scientists are beginning to argue the same. Both garlic and onion are rich in trace elements of aluminum, copper, iron, manganese, sulfur and zinc. Garlic contains crotonic aldehyde, a potent germ-killer.

Clove and cinnamon oils are chemically more powerful antiseptics than carbolic acid.

Coriander seed, nutmeg, mace and turmeric all aid digestion. Aniseed, cardamom, fennel and saffron are also recognized as aids to good digestion.

5

Indian Meals and How They Are Served

There are two main differences between dining in Indian and in Western style.

Indians do not use knives, forks or chopsticks. They use the fingers of the right hand and a ball of rice or a bit of bread as a scoop. It takes great dexterity to eat this way without becoming messy, and we do not recommend it for your table.

Also, in Western homes a meal usually consists of a main dish with surrounding side dishes, some of which may be served in turn. Indian meals are also built around one major dish, but all the dishes of the meal are always served at the same time.

Meals are served in different ways in different parts of India, but we suggest you follow the Bombay Palace menu which has been designed for Western diners.

The Bombay Palaces are famous for their luncheon buffets, where, for a fixed price, one may sample an entire range of Indian delicacies, including at least a dozen cold salads and vegetables, several curries, plus tandoor chicken and an endless quantity of fresh-baked nan. If you wish to follow this procedure for a party, simply choose several hot and cold appetizer dishes, and surround them with a few hot dishes, including at least one rice dish and one dal.

For family dining, you can use the Bombay Palace menu as a guide. Plan on one main dish (we Westerners are committed to a lot of meat), and prepare several side dishes that will complement it. By all means serve some form of bread, and always some form of rice.

In planning your menus, pay attention to both the colors and the textures of the dishes you are assembling.

To Indians, dining is almost a ritual, and cooks are greatly concerned with how the food looks; aesthetic pleasure is almost as much a part of dining as the taste of the foods.

A typical Indian family meal might consist of one rice dish, a dal or two, a vegetable or two and one major dish. Breads always accompany the foods. Chutneys and pickles are also always on hand to add additional spicing. These should combine sweet, tart, suave, and sour. For an easy rule of thumb as to how many dishes should be served at a meal, plan on twice the number of dishes as there are diners.

In India, the same dish may be served either hot or at room temperature. Some recipes in this book suggest that the dish be prepared in advance and allowed to cool for several hours before being reheated. This procedure melds the flavors better. As these examples show, while food in India is treated with great respect and tradition, there is also great leeway for individual expression and style.

Food Preparation and Equipment

The preparation of food in India is almost sacred. In some kitchens a circle is drawn on the floor beyond which only the cooks can pass. Food is handed to servers who stand outside the magic circle. There are beautiful stories about food, one of which tells of a prince who seeks for a wife a maiden who can stretch rice into a full meal. The description of how the young woman constructs the meal that wins the prince is both poetic and mouth watering.

But have no fear. With this book as a guide, food preparation will be demystified. Your kitchen probably contains everything you need to make the recipes in this book: no esoteric utensils are necessary.

The basic cooking utensil in the Indian kitchen is the *kadhai,* a metal vessel shaped very much like a wok. A wok makes a fine substitute. Otherwise use a deep skillet, either one of cast iron or a copper-clad stainless steel pan to spread heat rapidly and evenly. Nonstick Teflon or Silverstone type skillets are excellent for such things as frying onions and other vegetables.

Another utensil basic to an Indian kitchen is the *tava,* a slightly rounded griddle. Whatever you use to cook pancakes on will do admirably.

For the rest, you will do well to have a set of wooden spoons for stirring, a long-handled fork to lift cooked rice gently from the bottom of the pot so as not to crush the grains, and a slotted spoon to remove cooked food from hot fat.

Since Indian cookery depends on a great spectrum of herbs and spices, you will need a grinder. Indian cooks use a mortar and pestle for hand-grinding. Ideal for the purpose is a small electric grinder or even a small coffee grinder. Since spices are generally ground in tiny amounts, a blender is really too big, but you can get by with one.

Spices and herbs are rich in volatile oils, so they lose their fragrance and pungency quickly. Always buy in small quantities and store away from heat and light. If you have room for your spice jars in the refrigerator, that is a perfect place to store them.

DEBONING CHICKEN

Because the Indian cuisine is healthful, chicken is always skinned before using, and the fat removed. The meat can be left on the bone, which is most common, or deboned if you prefer. Although it is not a traditional Indian technique, we have found a way to debone a chicken quickly and easily:

Put a whole chicken in a pot and cover it with water. Bring the chicken to a boil, then set it aside to cool. At this point it is easy to peel off the meat, using your fingers, and to separate and discard the skin as well. The carcass can be further cooked, with an onion, some celery and a carrot, to make a nice chicken stock to be used for other purposes. If you use this method, the chicken will be partly cooked and can be finished in about half the time needed for a raw one.

CHILI PEPPERS

Much of Northern Indian cooking (the Punjabi Moghlai cuisine which forms the basis for most of the Bombay Palace kitchen recipes) is suave rather than fiery. Some Bengal dishes, many Madras dishes, nearly all Goa dishes, and cooking in the South in general, all make use of peppers of many kinds. As is true of all cultures, the closer to the equator the more hotly spiced are the dishes.

In this book the spice mixtures used give full flavor but are not expected to generate heat. Some of the Southern dishes, however, are fiery, as they should be. Even so, we have modified spiciness to suit the Western palate, albeit a sophisticated one. Indian cooking without spice is not Indian cooking.

To make shopping easier, we call for only a few of the countless types of peppers used in India, as follows:

RED PEPPER FLAKES   These fiery flakes, the same as you sprinkle on your pizza slices, are common in markets everywhere.

RED CHILI POWDER OR GROUND RED CHILI   This is the same as cayenne.

GREEN CHILIES   These small curling bright green chilies are available in many supermarkets and always in Indian, Latin or Oriental groceries. While they vary in size, a typical chili as called for in our recipes will be about 3 to 5 inches (8-13 cm) long, as thick as a man's thumb, and curved like a scimitar. The smaller they are the hotter they can be.

The Bombay Palace recipes usually call for one or two fresh green chilies, julienned or minced, with seeds left in. If you want a milder taste, slice open the chili and scrape out the seeds, for that is where the fire is. By seeding the chilies you can double the chili taste without doubling the heat. Wrapped loosely in a plastic bag, chilies will remain fresh in the refrigerator for about a week.

NOTE: It is wise to wear rubber gloves when handling fresh chili peppers of any sort. Otherwise, be sure not to touch your face until you have washed your hands well with soap and water. The chili oils can burn skin or eyes.

A NOTE ON FOOD COLORINGS USED IN INDIAN COOKING

In recent years there has rightly been some alarm about the potential health hazards of additives, and particularly some of the food dyes offered for sale, even in supermarkets.

Use of some food colorings is traditional in the Indian cuisine—for example, they are used to obtain the appetizing red color that dramatizes tandoori chicken.

A few recipes in this book call for such food colors. Omitting them will not alter the taste of the recipes, but it will affect their appearance. We have written to the department of Health and Human Services of the Food and Drug Administration about the colors mentioned in this book. The color additives called for are rated as follows:

FD&C Red #40 is listed as "permanently" approved for use in foods, drugs and cosmetics under our color-additive regulations.

FD&C Yellow #6 is permitted for use in foods, drugs and cosmetics.

FD&C Blue #1 may be safely used for coloring foods (including dietary supplements) generally in amounts consistent with good manufacturing practice.

A Guide to Special Ingredients

BASMATI RICE   A high quality long-grain rice used in Indian cooking that is slightly aromatic and nutlike in flavor. The rice should be picked over to remove any impurities. Also, basmati must be soaked at least 15 minutes before cooking. There is no finer rice than basmati, and nothing can truly take its place, but if you must use a substitute, regular long-grain rice is acceptable.

CARDAMOM (elaichi)   The fruit produced by a plant in the ginger family. Each pod contains from 15 to 20 seeds, which are widely used for flavoring. Most cardamom pods available in the United States are bleached, but Indian cooks prefer green cardamom. Indians also use the more assertive black cardamom pods.

COCONUT MILK   Liquid produced by mixing chopped coconut meat and water, then squeezing the pulp dry through cheesecloth. While the term is sometimes used to describe the natural liquid inside a coconut, that is not an ingredient in Indian cooking. (Indian name: *narial.*)

CORIANDER (channia)   An aromatic herb of the parsley family. While the seeds and the leafy greens of this plant have entirely different tastes, both are essential ingredients in Indian cooking. In the Bombay Palace kitchens, chopped fresh coriander leaves are used for both color and taste in almost every dish. There is no substitute for the taste of fresh coriander, although for color you can substitute flat-leaf (Italian) parsley. Fresh coriander can be obtained in most Indian, Chinese or Latin markets, and occasionally in American supermarkets. Dried coriander leaves have absolutely no flavor.

CUMIN SEED (jeera)   A strongly aromatic seed which reminds some people of caraway. Available whole or ground, it is widely used in India.

DAL   The Hindi name for all members of the legume or pulse family, including lentils, peas and dried beans.

GARAM MASALA   Fried spices, blended together in the home for use as seasoning. In this book, the term *full masala* indicates that the spices have been left whole. *Dry masala* means that the spices have been ground. Various commercial masala mixes can also be bought in Indian food shops and some "health food" stores. (Recipes pp. 15-19).

GHEE   Clarified butter, prepared by using a slow-cooking method. Unlike regular butter, it does not smoke when cooked at high temperatures. (Recipe on page 24.)

GINGER (adrak)   A pungent-tasting root. Fresh ginger should be used whenever possible. If absolutely necessary, $1/2$ teaspoon ground ginger can be substituted for a piece of fresh ginger the size of an almond, but expect inferior flavor.

ROSE WATER (gulab jal)   A liquid flavoring distilled from rose petals and used largely to flavor desserts.

TAMARIND (imli)   Edible brown pulp of a tropical seed pod. Both pulp (in cake form) and juice are used. Dried tamarind is valued for its natural sweet/sour taste. Lemon juice may be substituted.

TURMERIC (haldi)   Pungent spice of the ginger family. Fresh root turmeric is hard to obtain and difficult to grate. We recommend substituting powdered turmeric, which is used like saffron to color foods a golden yellow.

ASAFETIDA (hing)   A flavoring agent compounded of roots and plants that gives a dish an onionlike taste, it can be found in Indian and sometimes health-food shops in either powdered or gum form. (The gum form is easier to use because it is less pungent. Some Indian religious sects forbid onions in cooking because the flavor is considered too passionate, so asafetida is substituted. You can safely use onions.)

AMCHOOR POWDER   There is no English-language equivalent for this pungent flavoring agent, made from dried sour mango. Lemon juice is an acceptable substitute.

CHICK-PEA FLOUR (besan)   Ground chick-peas, or garbanzos, make a heavy flour much used in Indian cuisine. It is usually lightened by adding other flours.

FENNEL SEED (saunf)   An anise-flavored seed much used in Indian cooking.

FENUGREEK SEED (mehti)   As with coriander, the leaf and the seed have distinctly different characteristics, both delicious and both used. They can be obtained in powdered form in Indian and health-food shops.

Special Note to Users of the Metric System

Recipes in this book are designed to be used with either American standard measures or the metric system. For example:

2 pounds (1 kg) lean lamb
2 large onions
2 cups milk
1 tablespoon flour
1 3-inch (8-cm) cinnamon stick

It must be stressed that the metric quantities are not precisely the same as the American equivalent; we have rounded off measurements for ease of use. Using the metric system will produce proportionate recipes, but the final amount may be about 5 percent more.

Here are some examples of the equivalents used in the book:

1 kilogram (1 kg) = 2+ pounds
30 grams (30 gm) = 1 ounce
1 liter = 1+ quart (34 ounces)

Chapter 3

BASIC RECIPES
AND TECHNIQUES

Perhaps more than any other single factor, the use of spices distinguishes Indian cooking from the other great cuisines of the world. Accordingly, this chapter includes several recipes for spice mixtures that you will be using often.

Indian cooking also makes liberal use of sauces. While every recipe in this book naturally includes instructions for the sauce which is part of a given dish, we are also providing separate sauce recipes here; we recommend that you experiment with using these versatile and savory sauces in non-Indian cooking.

In addition, this chapter provides instructions for preparing key ingredients such as ghee and coconut milk, which are used in recipes throughout the book.

Bhoona—An Essential Technique

To *bhoona* is an essential of authentic Indian cooking. It is a technique not found in other cuisines, but in Western terms *bhoona*-ing resembles a combination of sauteing and braising. Reduction is a French technique that also comes close.

To *bhoona* a dish means to reduce the liquids to a "dry" state, to a kind of paste. A dry curry is one that has been *bhoona*-ed, so that there is little or no gravy. Actually, you can make additional gravy simply by *bhoona*-ing first and then adding a small quantity of water. A good Indian chef always keeps a cup of water handy so that he can sprinkle a few drops of water into the pot if a *bhoona*-ed mixture has neared the scorching point.

There are two reasons for using the *bhoona* technique. Since Indians eat without knife, fork or spoon, and use a bit of bread or a little mound of rice as a scoop, it is easier to manage a "dry" dish than one with lots of gravy. *Bhoona*-ing is also an important technique at the stove because drying the mixture by constant stirring over high heat encourages all of the spices and juices to enter the meat or vegetables to give them the fullest flavor.

The *bhoona* technique means that the meat mixture is cooked over medium-high heat, with constant stirring to avoid scorching, until all liquids are reduced and the spices coat the meat like a paste. About $1/2$ cup of water can then be added, the dish covered, and a gravy created as the dish becomes reliquified again.

Here is a simple master recipe for the technique:

1. Heat the oil or butter.

2. Add the the spices called for, and stir-fry over medium-high or high heat until a paste is formed. This often takes only $1/2$ minute.

3. Add the meat mixture and stir to coat meat well with the spice paste.

4. Add the dry masala and—if the recipe does not call for a wet vegetable such as tomato—add $1/2$ cup water.

5. Bhoona again for 15-20 minutes.

6. If you wish more sauce, add $1/4$ cup water, cover, and simmer 5 minutes.

IMPORTANT NOTE: When *bhoona*-ing, it may be necessary to sprinkle meat mixture with a few drops of water to keep it from scorching.

Spice and Seasoning Mixtures

GARAM MASALA means "dry spice mixture." There are many types of garam masala, which combine spices in different proportions. When garam masala is packaged for sale to Western countries, it is usually labelled "curry powder". However, Indian food shops also carry several different spice mixtures labelled garam masala, but these gentle seasonings should not be confused with the garam masalas prepared at home. They are intended for different purposes, for example, for sprinkling on already prepared dishes to add a bit of zest just prior to serving.

Commercial curry powders often combine several garam masalas into one all-purpose mixture. True Indian cooks always make up their own spice mixtures, to add their personal stamp to otherwise classic dishes. We urge you to do the same. If you must buy a commercial curry powder, avoid insipid domestic blends (which too often contain mostly turmeric, used as carrying agent for a few tame spices), and buy an imported mixture from an Indian shop.

CURRY PASTE is a prepackaged curry mixture that has oil and possibly other liquids added to form a paste.

SAMBAR POWDER is another traditional spice blend. In Southern India, sambar powder substitutes for garam masala. (Moghul cooking, the kind in which the Bombay Palace kitchens specialize, uses garam masala, either full or dry).

FULL MASALA is a term used in this book to signify that the spices used are left whole.

DRY MASALA means that the spices have been ground.

You will note from the recipe printed here that sambar powder is a much "hotter" blend; Southern India enjoys its food much spicier than the North. Note that "sambar" also has a different meaning: a kind of vegetable stew. In Eastern India there is another quite popular version of garam masala that is called panch phoron. This comes from the Madras region, where the inhabitants also like their food highly spiced.

Recipes for several types of "dry spice mixtures" are given on the following pages. Being freshly ground, they will have more flavor than premixed masalas bought in a store. All the garam masala recipes that follow can be used interchangeably in all our recipes. Select the one you prefer, or even invent one all your own.

Garam Masala—Blend #1

Roast the following spices in a skillet over medium heat for 3-5 minutes, until they begin hopping and start to change color. Do not scorch.

MAKES ABOUT 1 CUP

OUNCES		GRAMS
2	coriander seeds	60
2	cumin seeds	60
2	fenugreek	60
1	poppy seeds	30
1	black peppercorns	30
1/2	yellow mustard seeds	15

Put the seeds into a blender or mortar. Add:

4	ground turmeric	120
1	ground ginger	30
1	red pepper flakes	30

Blend mixture well. Store in a dark place in an airtight container. Use 1 or 2 rounded tablespoons for a curry dish for four people.

Garam Masala—Blend #II (Spicy)

Put the following spices, dry, in a skillet and over medium heat roast them 3-5 minutes until they start to change color. Do not scorch.

MAKES ABOUT 1 CUP

OUNCES		GRAMS
8	coriander seeds	240
2	dried red chili flakes	60
2	black peppercorns	60
2	yellow mustard seeds	60
1	cumin seeds	30

Put the roasted seeds into a blender or a mortar. Add:

2	ground turmeric	60
2	salt	60
2	sugar	60
1	ground ginger	30

Blend mixture until spices are completely pulverized. Store in a dark place in an airtight container. Use 1 or 2 rounded tablespoons for a curry dish for four people.

Kashmiri Garam Masala— Blend #III

3 dried chilies, or 1 teaspoon pepper flakes
6 tablespoons coriander seeds
1 tablespoon peppercorns
1 teaspoon cumin seeds
1 teaspoon fenugreek
1 teaspoon mustard seeds
4 cloves

In a wok or heavy skillet roast the spices over high heat until there is a slight color change—about 3 minutes. Do not let the spices scorch. Grind the mixture to a fine powder and keep in an airtight jar.

For each recipe for four persons, use about 1 rounded tablespoon of the blend.

Kashmiri Garam Masala— Blend #IV

10 1-inch pieces cinnamon stick (10 3-cm pieces)
24 cloves
1 teaspoon cumin seeds
1/2 teaspoon grated nutmeg
8 pods black cardamom

In a wok or heavy skillet roast the spices over medium heat until there is a slight color change—about 3 minutes.

Do not let spices scorch. Grind the mixture to a fine powder and keep in an airtight jar.

For a dish serving four, use about 1 rounded tablespoon of the blend.

Garam Masala—#V
A Goa Variation

This is an old-time recipe for a garam masala intended as a starter for Duck Vindaloo, but it can be used in other types of curries as well.

MAKES ENOUGH FOR ONE CURRY SERVING 4-6 PERSONS

Put the following spices, dry, in a skillet, and over medium heat roast them 3 to 5 minutes, until they begin to dance and start to change color. Do not scorch.

2 teaspoons dried red chilies
1 teaspoon coriander seeds
1/2 teaspoon cumin seeds
12 peppercorns
5 cloves
4 cardamom pods
3 bay leaves

Put the roasted seeds and cardamom pods into a blender or mortar. Add:

1 3-inch (8 cm) cinnamon stick, crushed
1 tablespoon ground ginger

Blend mixture until completely pulverized. Store powder in a dark place in an airtight container. Use 1 or 2 rounded tablespoons for a curry dish serving four people.

Sambar Podi
SAMBAR POWDER

Sambar powder is a type of garam masala very popular in Madras and the South of India (see also Panch Phoron, opposite). It is similar to other garam masalas except that it is considerably spicier, in accordance with South Indian taste. Sometimes a dish will be called a sambar, indicating that it is a vegetable mixture spiced with sambar powder. Sambar can also be bought ready-made.

MAKES ABOUT 1 CUP

3 tablespoons black peppercorns
6 tablespoons coriander seeds
5 red chilies, crushed
1 tablespoon turmeric
1 tablespoon mustard seed
1 tablespoon cumin seeds
1 tablespoon fenugreek seeds

In a wok or heavy skillet toast the spices until they begin to dance and change color. Do not scorch. Grind them in a spice mill or blender, and store in an airtight container. Use about 1 tablespoon sambar per recipe for four, or more as desired.

Panch Phoron

This Eastern region five-spice blend can be used as a substitute for garam masala. Panch phoron is usually added to a dish just toward the end of cooking, to enhance the flavors of vegetables or a stew. Panch means "five", and panch phoron means "land of five rivers". (The Jhelum, Beas, Ravi, Chenab and Sutlej combine to form the Indus River.)

Panch Phoron #I

Combine these spices in equal amounts:

mustard seeds
aniseeds
cumin seeds
powdered cinnamon
red chilies, crushed

You can use this mixture either whole or ground, according to taste.

Panch Phoron #II

Combine these spices in equal amounts:

powdered cinnamon
black cumin seeds
cumin seeds
fenugreek seeds
mustard seeds

Use this mixture either whole or ground according to taste.

Stendahl's 15-Spice Curry Powder

Indians export garam masalas labelled as curry powder, with a bow to Western innocence. While it is strongly recommended that you compound your own different types of garam masalas—preferably fresh each time you cook Indian cuisine—this 15-spice curry powder has served me remarkably well.

I have given this curry powder to many Indian friends, all of whom have declared it excellent. Perhaps because it is made of so many wonderful spices and herbs, it has a complexity that makes it a "universal" garam masala. Ground in advance and kept in airtight jars away from sunlight, the powder retains its fragrance and pungency for many months. Be sure to buy the spices from a store that sells only fresh ingredients. Using a blender, or preferably an electric spice mill (or coffee grinder set to finest grind), pulverize the following ingredients:

OUNCES		GRAMS
8	powdered turmeric	240
8	coriander seeds	240
8	cumin seeds	240
6	powdered ginger	180
4	black peppercorns	120
1	powdered cardamom seeds	30
2	fennel seeds	60
2	small dried red peppers	60
2	powdered mace	60
1	whole cloves	30
1	yellow mustard seeds	30
1	poppy seeds	30
1	garlic powder	30
1	fenugreek seeds	30
1/2	powdered cinnamon	15

Store airtight in several small jars. Dark glass or ceramic jars are the best.

Garlic/Ginger Paste

This delightfully pungent paste is called for in many Moghul style recipes, and is an essential condiment in the Bombay Palace kitchens. You need not confine the use of garlic/ginger paste to Indian cooking; try it on meat and vegetable dishes from other cuisines.

It can be made fresh each time, using equal amounts of garlic and ginger as follows:

MAKES 1 ROUNDED TABLESPOON:

3 small garlic cloves, mashed
piece of fresh ginger, size of walnut, peeled and minced

MAKES 1 ROUNDED TEASPOON:

1 small garlic clove, mashed
piece of fresh ginger, size of almond, peeled and minced

Grind the ingredients together, adding a drop of water to make a smooth paste. Use a mortar and pestle or a blender.

If you plan to do any amount of Indian cooking in the near future, it will save you time to make a larger quantity of the paste and store it in a screw-top jar in the refrigerator. The paste keeps well this way.

MAKES 1/2 CUP:

10 cloves garlic
piece of fresh ginger, the size of a baby carrot, about 3 inches long
by 1 1/2-inch thick (8 cm × 4 cm)

Blend to a smooth paste and keep in tightly sealed jar in the refrigerator.

Butters, Cheese and Yoghurt

Ghee
CLARIFIED BUTTER

Indians in the North use ghee for their cooking, Southern Indians prefer mustard oil, which is very spicy and better suits their preference for highly seasoned foods. Ghee made from butter is expensive, so many modern households use a vegetable ghee, somewhat similar to Western margarine.

Ghee is clarified butter, but in India it is made differently from the French method, which is simply to melt sweet butter and then pour off the solids. All clarified butter is useful in the kitchen because it has a higher smoking point than ordinary butter, and it also will keep longer, even without refrigeration.

In the Bombay Palace kitchens, ghee is used in large quantities, and prepared according to the following time-saving method:

Bring a pound ($^1/_2$ kg) of sweet butter to a boil. Set aside to cool. Use until the sediment at the bottom is reached, then discard and start with fresh butter. A shallow pan of this fast-method ghee is always ready at the chef's stove at the Bombay Palace.

The Bombay Palace kitchen recipe is a simple, excellent way to make ghee. While the majority of recipes in this book call for sweet butter rather than ghee, naturally the more authentic ingredient can be used instead. Remember, if you do use sweet butter, which has a lower smoking point than ghee, care must be taken not to allow it to brown in the pan.

NOTE: For recipes in this book that call for oil, use any light vegetable oil such as peanut oil or sunflower oil, but never olive oil. If you prefer, use a mixture of half sweet butter and half oil. This produces a mixture with a higher smoking point than butter alone, yet still gives butter flavor.

Tardka
SCENTED BUTTER

Tardka is butter spiced with fragrant and/or pungent herbs and spices of the cook's choice. It is used to flavor bland dishes such as dals and other vegetables. Use your imagination to create your personal tardka, or try this one, as often prepared in the Bombay Palace kitchens.

MAKES 4 SERVINGS

4 tablespoons butter (¹/₂ stick, 60 gm)
1¹/₂ teaspoons powdered cumin

1 large onion, chopped fine
¹/₂ cup heavy cream
2 tablespoons chopped coriander leaves

1. In a wok or heavy skillet, melt butter over medium flame. Add the cumin seeds. When they begin to brown, about 10 seconds, add the onions and stir constantly until onions begin to brown, about 8 minutes. Do not let the mixture scorch.

2. Remove from heat, quickly stir in the cream and coriander leaves and spoon over any dal or other vegetable dish.

NOTE: Black mustard seeds, cloves, ginger root or chilies can also be added, singly or in combination. Sour cream or yoghurt can be used instead of heavy cream. Create your own personal tardka.

Dahi
YOGHURT

Before you attempt to make yoghurt at home, try to find a source that sells an Eastern style, homemade type. It is amazingly different in texture and taste from the commercial stuff in paper containers. Once you find a creamy yoghurt you like, you can use it as a starter to make your own. By saving a little each time for the next batch, you can make your own yoghurt forever.

MAKES 1 QUART

1 quart homogenized milk
2 tablespoons top-quality yoghurt, the freshest possible

1. Bring milk to boiling point, stirring with a wooden spoon to prevent formation of a skin. When the milk begins to rise in the pan, remove from heat and let cool to lukewarm. (The ideal temperature is 115° F. If the temperature is too hot, it will kill the yoghurt culture; if too cool, the yoghurt will set but it will take much longer.)

2. While milk is warming, smear the yoghurt starter around inside a ceramic bowl. A kitchen table is fine in summer weather, otherwise set the bowl in an oven that has a pilot light and shut the door. Let it stand overnight. When the yoghurt has set, store in the refrigerator. For best flavor, it should be used within 3 days.

Paneer
HOMEMADE INDIAN CHEESE

Paneer, besides being eaten by itself or as an accompaniment to food, is also called for in certain recipes. (See Saag Paneer, p. 136.) When it is pressed into cake form it is called *paneer*; when left in curd form it is called *channa*. Certainly it is best to make your own fresh paneer for these recipes, but it is possible to substitute farmer's cheese, or even ricotta, if you wrap the cheese in cheesecloth and press out the liquid.

2 quarts (2 liters) milk
1/2 cup white vinegar

1. In a wok or heavy saucepan, bring milk to boil over high heat. Add the vinegar and stir constantly until the milk curdles.

2. Strain through a piece of heavy cheesecloth, then fold the cheesecloth up to form a bag. Tie the bag securely and flatten it under a heavy weight. This can be done by putting the cheese bag in a heavy pot and putting a weight of several books or other objects on top of it.

3. Set the cheese bag in a cool place for 3 or 4 hours, until the cheese is firm. It should form a mass about 1/2 to 1 inch thick (about 2 cm).

4. Open the cloth and cut the paneer into 1 1/2 by 1 inch squares (about 3 cm by 2 cm).

5. Deep fry until golden. Drain and set aside for later use.

Sauces and Gravies

In this book each recipe includes its own sauce made from scratch. Obviously, in a large modern restaurant kitchen, many sauces are made in advance and kept at stoveside for immediate use or blending.

The Bombay Palace maintains a reserve of three major sauces:

BUTTER TOMATO SAUCE   A thick, rich sauce used for these Bombay Palace classics: Butter Chicken, Murgh Masala, Paneer Makhani. Bombay Palace chefs will often add a spoonful of this elixir to enliven almost any kind of gravy except the white sauce.

CURRY SAUCE   A meduim-thick sauce for any curried poultry, meats or vegetables.

BADAMI SAUCE   Used for Shrimp, Fish Badami, Lamb Pasanda, Murgh Shahi Korma. Badami is a white sauce and the lightest of the three.

In addition to the three major sauces, the chef also keeps on hand his garlic/ginger paste, his onion sauce, his melted butter and his heavy cream, as well as various ground condiments, and of course a large supply of fresh chopped coriander. From all of these seasonings and ingredients, a good chef can make 1,001 variations, and still keep within the classical tradition.

Basic Butter Tomato Sauce

In the Bombay Palace kitchens this savory sauce is made up in quantity, and a spoonful or two is often used to enrich many dishes. This is the basic sauce for dishes such as Bhindi Masala, Boti Kabab Masala, Matter Paneer, Murgh Tikka, and of course, Butter Chicken.

*2 pounds (1 kg) tomatoes,
   pureed in blender (about 4
   cups)*
*1 6-ounce (180 gm) can
   tomato paste*
8 ounces (240 gm) butter
*1 tablespoon fenugreek
   powder*

Dry Masala:
1 tablespoon paprika
1 teaspoon ground cardamom
1 teaspoon red chili powder
¹/₂ teaspoon salt
generous grinding of pepper

1 teaspoon sugar

In a wok or heavy skillet over a medium-high flame, *bhoona* the pureed tomatoes, tomato paste, butter, dry masala, and sugar. *Bhoona* over medium-high heat until thick enough to coat a spoon, about 5-7 minutes.

NOTE: This is a basic sauce, parallel to a demi-glaze in Western cooking. It can be used as is, or to finish other dishes.

   To finish a dish of poultry, meat, paneer or vegetables, using Butter Tomato Sauce as a base:

*6 tablespoons butter tomato
   sauce (¹/₃ cup; 70 ml)*
¹/₄ teaspoon ground cumin
¹/₄ teaspoon paprika
generous grinding of pepper
*1 fresh green chili, quartered
   and sliced into matchsticks*
*1 tablespoon garlic/ginger
   paste, or*

3 garlic cloves, mashed
*1 piece fresh ginger, size of
   walnut, minced*
4 tablespoons heavy cream
*2 cups cooked ingredients
   such as: lamb cubes,
   tandoori chicken, paneer or
   vegetables*

1. In a wok or heavy skillet, heat the butter tomato sauce over medium-high heat. Add the spices, the garlic/ginger paste and the green chili, *bhoona*-ing so the sauce does not scorch.

2. Add the meat or vegetables and continue *bhoona*-ing, making sure the mixture does not stick. Add ¹/₄ cup water if sauce becomes too thick. Stir constantly.

3. Add the heavy cream and half the coriander, and keep stirring until sauce bubbles. Garnish with the remaining coriander, and serve at once.

NOTE: If butter begins to separate out of sauce, add more cream; keep stirring until butter is thoroughly incorporated.

Basic Curry Sauce To Be Used with Leftovers

This is a useful sauce for dressing already cooked meats and vegetables.

3 medium onions, coarsely
   chopped and pureed in
   blender with a bit of water
1 large tomato, skinned
1 tablespoon garlic/ginger
   paste, or
   3 cloves garlic, mashed,
   1 piece fresh ginger, size of
     walnut, minced
$^1/_4$ cup oil
1 3-inch (8 cm) cinnamon
   stick, broken

Full Masala:
4 whole cloves
2 green cardamom pods,
   crushed
2 black cardamom pods,
   crushed
1 teaspoon dried chili flakes

$^1/_2$ teaspoon cumin seeds
$^1/_2$ teaspoon coriander seeds
2 bay leaves
generous grinding of pepper

Dry Masala:
1 teaspoon garam masala
1 teaspoon paprika
$^1/_2$ teaspoon red chili powder
$^1/_2$ teaspoon ground coriander
   powder
$^1/_2$ teaspoon turmeric
$^1/_2$ teaspoon ground cumin
$^1/_2$ teaspoon salt

1 cup water
2 ounces (60 gm) cashew
   ground to a paste
4 cups leftover meat, poultry,
   fish, vegetables or paneer
2 ounces (60 ml) heavy cream

1. Prepare the onions, garlic/ginger paste, and the tomatoes.

2. In a wok or heavy skillet heat the oil over medium-high flame. Add the full masala and *bhoona* 30 seconds. Add the onion puree and the ginger/garlic paste and *bhoona*, stirring constantly, until the puree begins to turn brown. Stir in the tomatoes, and *bhoona* a few minutes until the mixture thickens.

3. Add the dry masala and *bhoona* 2 minutes. Add 1 cup of water, reduce heat, and simmer until mixture is thick enough to coat a spoon, about 10 minutes.

4. Add the cashew paste and *bhoona* 5 minutes, stirring to avoid scorching.

5. Add the meat or vegetables to sauce and heat well. Add heavy cream, simmer 3 minutes, and serve.

NOTE: This mixture freezes well for a month or more.

Badami Sauce

This is a somewhat delicate white sauce that goes well with fish and light meats and many kinds of leftovers.

3 medium-sized onions,
   pureed in blender
1/4 cup oil
4 ounces (120 gm) fresh
   yoghurt
3 ounces (90 gm) blanched
   sliced almonds
3 ounces (90 gm) cashews,
   ground with a bit of water
   to make a paste

Dry Masala:
1/2 teaspoon ground
   cardamom
1/2 teaspoon ground mace
1/2 teaspoon fresh-ground
   nutmeg
1/2 teaspoon salt
generous grinding of pepper
   (white preferred)

2 cups milk
1 cup heavy cream

1. Prepare the onions and set aside. Prepare the nut paste and set aside.

2. In a wok or heavy skillet, heat the oil over medium heat and add the onion puree. Stir 5 minutes, but do not let the onions color. Add the yoghurt and stir gently for 5 minutes. Add the nut paste, lower heat, and stir gently for 10 minutes.

3. Add the dry masala and simmer gently 5 minutes.

4. Add the milk and simmer 10 minutes.

5. Just before serving, add the heavy cream and simmer until heated through, 3 minutes. The sauce is now ready for use.

6. When adding leftovers, allow 1 cup solids per person. The solid ingredients must be heated in the sauce before adding the heavy cream.

Onion Gravy

This is a basic sauce much used in the Bombay Palace kitchens, somewhat akin to the stock and demi-glaze of Western cooking. Onion gravy is added to many dishes to thicken them and increase their zestiness. Make it ahead in quantity and freeze what you do not use right away. You will find onion gravy has many uses other than for Indian cooking.

MAKES ABOUT 2 CUPS OF GRAVY

1 pound (¹/₂ kg) onions,
    coarsely chopped
2 tablespoons butter

Dry Masala:
1 teaspoon paprika
¹/₂ teaspoon ground cumin
¹/₂ teaspoon ground coriander

¹/₂ teaspoon turmeric
¹/₄ teaspoon red chili powder
1 teaspoon garam masala
1 teaspoon salt, and generous
    grinding of pepper

2 tomatoes, chopped
4 large cashews

1. Put the chopped onions in a blender or food processor and add a little water. Blend to a paste. Do not clean blender.

2. In a wok or heavy skillet melt the butter and add the onion paste. *Bhoona*, stirring constantly over medium heat, about 20 minutes to "dry" the onions. Do not let them scorch.

3. Add the dry marsala and the salt and pepper and *bhoona* 3 minutes. Add the chopped tomatoes and enough water to make a thick gravy, about 1 cup. Simmer over low heat.

4. In the blender puree the cashews with a bit of water to make a paste. Scrape out the paste and add it to the gravy. Simmer for 10 minutes.

Basic Onion and Tomato Sauce

This onion-tomato sauce can be used as the base for many different kinds of curries. When used with meat, fish or vegetables, it is sometimes finished with heavy cream. This sauce is also delicious when used for non-Indian cooking.

MAKES ABOUT 2 CUPS

3 medium onions, minced by hand or ground with a bit of water in a blender
3 large tomatoes, crushed
1/4 cup oil

Full Masala:
1 teaspoon green cardamom pods, crushed
1 teaspoon black cardamom pods, crushed
8 whole cloves
2 tablespoons garlic/ginger paste, or

4 garlic cloves, mashed
fresh ginger, size of a Brazil nut, minced

Dry Masala:
1/2 teaspoon each of the following spices, ground:
cinnamon
coriander
fenugreek
garam masala
nutmeg
red chili powder
turmeric

1. Prepare onions and tomatoes and set aside.

2. In a wok or heavy skillet, heat the oil. Add the full masala and *bhoona* 30 seconds. Add the onions and *bhoona* over medium-high heat until they begin to turn brown, about 5 minutes.

3. Add the ginger/garlic paste and the dry masala and *bhoona* 3 minutes. Add the crushed tomatoes, turn heat to low, and simmer until thickened, about 15 minutes. Stir constantly to prevent scorching.

Onion Sauce

In the Bombay Palace kitchens this versatile flavor enhancer is always kept stoveside to be added to any number of dishes. You will find it useful for other than Indian cooking.

MAKES 1 CUP

1 tablespoon oil
3 onions, chopped fine
2 garlic cloves, mashed
1 piece fresh ginger, size of almond, minced

Heat oil in wok or heavy skillet. Add onions and cook over medium heat, stirring constantly, until onions are translucent, 6 to 7 minutes. The onions must always remain soft, so it may be necessary to add a spoonful or so of water to keep them moist as they cook.

Coconut Milk

This infusion is a frequent ingredient in Indian cooking, and especially in Southern India, where it is used to thicken curries and other dishes. The first infusion is called thick coconut milk, and the second infusion, thin coconut milk. Begin by selecting a heavy coconut and shake it to make sure that it is full of juice. A full coconut is a fresh one.

1. Pierce the "eyes" of the coconut with a nail or skewer. Pour out the juice for drinking, or discard.

2. Put the coconut in a preheated 375° F oven for 15 minutes. Remove and put the coconut on a board. Strike coconut sharply with a hammer; the coconut will break in two and the shell will come away from the flesh.

3. With a sharp knife, pare out the meat of the skin, and grate the pieces into a bowl.

4. Bring 3 cups of water to a boil, and pour it over the coconut. Set aside to cool for 30 minutes.

5. Pour the coconut milk through a strainer lined with cheesecloth. Squeeze the pulp to get as much liquid as possible. A second infusion may be made by adding another 2 cups of boiling water and reheating the straining. *Alternate method:* The coconut mixture may be placed in blender and processed at high speed before straining through cheesecloth.

NOTE: Coconut cream in cans, widely available in supermarkets, must be diluted. If you do not make your own, dissolve ½ cup of canned coconut cream in 1 ½ cups boiling water before using.

Chapter 4

MASTER DEMONSTRATION RECIPES: A MINI COOKING COURSE IN INDIAN CUISINE

We have chosen two of the most popular recipes from the Bombay Palace menu and have analyzed each step of their preparation in great detail.

The actual working recipes appear in their concise form elsewhere in the book, but here we have presented them with complete instructions and explanation in order to teach general principles of Indian cooking—not merely how to prepare a specific dish.

If you master only these two recipes, you will be able to prepare many similar dishes with ease. By using any meat of your choice, or even substituting vegetables for meat and following the recipes step by step, you will be able to create an endless series of authentic Punjabi style dishes. Again, you can lend your own personal accent to either the full masala, the dry masala, or both, simply by altering the quantities or even substituting one of your favorite spices for those in the recipe.

Thus the mastery of these two recipes and the necessary cooking techniques will enable you to improvise on classical themes, adapt recipes to your own taste, and even create new ones!

A Bombay Palace Chicken Curry

This recipe presents a classic example of Punjabi style poultry cooking, which is a specialty of the Bombay Palace kitchens.

MAIN INGREDIENTS

1. One 3-pound chicken, skinned and cut into 8 pieces (1.5 kg)
Indian food is healthful, not only because of the natural spices used, but because all fat is trimmed from meats: with poultry, both skin and fat are carefully removed.

TO SKIN A CHICKEN: Using one hand, grasp the chicken with a napkin or dishcloth to hold securely. With the other hand, insert fingers between the skin and the body at the neck opening and peel the skin back, cutting with a knife where necessary to separate it from the flesh.

Wing tips and the webbing between the lower ribs and the tail are also removed. The skin and these chicken parts can be used later in the stock pot. Chicken wings can be made into cocktail snacks or used as salad ingredients at another time. Chicken bones can be left in or removed, as you prefer.

TO BONE A CHICKEN: Put a whole chicken in a pot and cover it with water. Bring to the boil, then set aside to cool. When cooled, the meat can easily be picked away from the bones and saved for later uses, as can the poaching stock.

If you use this method the chicken will be partially cooked, and can be finished in approximately half the time required for cooking a raw chicken.

CUT CHICKEN INTO 8 PIECES. This is a natural division of the chicken meat. In the Bombay Palace kitchens, after the bird has been skinned a chef places the bird breast-side down, and cuts it horizontally with one stroke of a sharp knife, dividing the breast half from the rear half. Then the wing tips are severed by knife or cleaver, the wings are cut at the joints; the breast is divided into two parts, and the legs also divided at the joints.

2. 3 tomatoes
In some cuisines, tomatoes are seeded and skinned. Indians enjoy the difference in the textures and also consider using the entire tomato to be more healthful.

3. Full masala:

> *3-inch piece cinnamon stick, broken in pieces (8 cm)*
> *4 black cardamom pods, crushed*
> *6 green cardamom pods, crushed*

(While black cardamoms add their distinct flavor, they are not always easy to obtain. You can substitute by using 8 green cardamom pods to give an equivalent flavor boost.)

> *6 whole cloves*
> *2 dried red chilies, crushed (or substitute*
> *1 teaspoon red pepper flakes)*
> *¹/₂ teaspoon cumin seed, crushed*

Masala means a blend of spices. Garam means a blend of "warm" spices. It is common in Indian cooking to use a blend of spices in two different ways in the same dish. To simplify recipes for Western household use, we have divided the spice blends as follows:

Full masala—Whole spices or cracked spices. These are usually added to heated oil and cooked a few seconds to release their aromatic treasures before other ingredients are added. Or some cooks choose to increase the flavor of the masala by roasting the raw spices and seeds in a pan over low heat (or 15 minutes in a 300°F oven) before crushing them. The spices must not be allowed to scorch—when they begin to change color or to hop around in the pan, it is time to remove them, to be crushed coarsely.

Dry masala—and *garam masala*—will be explained below.

4. ¹/₄ cup oil
Note: Northern Indians prefer ghee, a form of clarified butter which keeps well without refrigeration. Southern Indians prefer oil, frequently mustard oil, which adds an increased hotness to dishes which Indians in the South enjoy. Butter-based ghee is expensive, so many Indians at home use a vegetable-derived ghee, similar to our margarine (see p. 24).

Indians like to use plenty of oil. After cooking, they remove the excess to be re-used later. In this book we suggest less oil for the recipes as a bow to Western tastes; if there is any surplus oil when a dish is finished, by all means reserve it for later use.

5. 3 onions, chopped fine

6. 1 tablespoon garlic/ginger paste, or 3 garlic cloves, mashed, and 1 piece fresh ginger, size of a walnut, minced

Garlic/ginger paste is often used in Bombay Palace recipes. If you intend to do Indian cooking once a week or more, it makes sense to prepare garlic/ginger paste in quantity (see p. 23) and use it by the spoonful as needed. You will find garlic/ginger paste adds a delightful flavor to vegetable and other dishes in Western cuisines as well.

7. Salt and fresh-ground pepper to taste
The masalas and other spices used in Indian cooking add so much flavor that less salt can be used than ordinarily. Pepper should always be fresh-ground for each recipe.

8. Dry Masala:

$1^1/_2$ *teaspoon ground coriander*
1 teaspoon ground cumin
1 teaspoon turmeric
$^1/_2$ *teaspoon red chili powder*

Dry masala, usually added after *bhoona*-ing (see p. 13) often echoes the full masala, but in powder form, the whole spices enter the meat during the first stage of cooking; the dry masala adds flavor to the sauce. Again, inventive cooks vary the ingredients of the dry masala according to personal taste.

9. $^1/_2$ cup yoghurt

10. 1 rounded tablespoon tomato paste

11. 4 tablespoons heavy cream

12. 1 tablespoon garam masala
Garam masala is a mixture of spices which Western cooks call curry powder. In Indian stores there are several different types of commercially prepared garam masalas. Garam masalas are excellent sprinkled over a completed dish just prior to serving. When you use the full and dry masala recommended in these recipes, you can get by without adding commercial garam masala. Adding such a blend at the last moment merely lends an extra dash of flavor.

13. 2 tablespoons coriander leaves, chopped

Many chefs, including those at the Bombay Palace kitchens, like to add a touch of bright green coriander leaves to garnish almost every dish and to add their own interesting taste. Chopped parsley may be substituted for looks, but the taste will not be the same.

SUMMARY OF INGREDIENTS FOR BOMBAY PALACE CHICKEN CURRY

SERVES 4-6

3-pound chicken, skinned and cut into 8 pieces (1½ kg)
3 tomatoes, diced

Full Masala:
¼ cup oil
3 onions, chopped fine
1 tablespoon garlic/ginger paste, or
  2 garlic cloves, mashed and 1 piece of ginger, size of a walnut, minced

salt and fresh-ground pepper to taste

Dry Masala:
½ cup yoghurt
1 rounded tablespoon tomato paste
4 tablespoons heavy cream
1 tablespoon garam masala
2 tablespoons coriander leaves, chopped

METHOD:
1. Prepare the chicken; set aside.

2. Dice the tomatoes; set aside.

3. In a wok or heavy skillet, heat the oil and add the full masala, stirring well for ½ minute. Add onions and stir-fry until they start to turn golden. Add garlic/ginger paste and *bhoona* over medium high heat to dry the mixture. Add the chicken and tomatoes and the dry masala. *Bhoona* for 5 minutes, adding a bit of water if necessary to prevent scorching. Add the

yoghurt, reduce heat and *bhoona* for 10-15 minutes while the chicken absorbs the spices, again adding a bit of water if necessary to avoid scorching.

4. This dish is classically a "dry" curry, but if you prefer more gravy, add ½ cup water at this point, and simmer for 5 minutes more.

5. Add the tomato paste and the heavy cream. Sprinkle on the garam masala, if desired, and garnish with the coriander leaves. Serve hot with rice.

Lamb Curry, Punjabi Style

This recipe presents a classic example of Punjabi style meat cooking which is a specialty of the Bombay Palace kitchens. It also demonstrates how, while a cook follows tradition in executing the recipe, he can personalize it by varying certain ingredients according to his own taste.

By using any meat of your choice, or even substituting vegetables for meat, and following this recipe step by step, you will be able to create an endless series of dishes in an authentic Punjabi style. Again, you can lend your own personal accent to either the full masala, the dry masala, or both, simply by altering the quantities or even substituting favored spices for others. This clearly shows how an Indian cook can follow a traditional recipe and yet make the dish his own.

NOTE: While generally main-dish recipes are planned to serve 4 persons, if you add one or more vegetable dishes to the meal, the main dish will serve more people.

MAIN INGREDIENTS

1. 2 pounds baby lamb, all fat removed, boned, and cut into 2-inch cubes (5 cm)
NOTE: Meat is always trimmed of all fat, and chicken trimmed of fat and also completely skinned. This is one reason why Indian cooking is so healthful.

2. 2 potatoes, peeled, each cut into 4 pieces

3. 1/2 cup oil

NOTE: Indians sometimes use oil, sometimes ghee, clarified butter, regular butter, or—in the South of India, where food is spicier—mustard oil.

Indians like to use plenty of oil, then drain off excess. You can make your own adjustment.

4. 2 medium onions cut in thin half-rings (see Do Piaza, p. 68)

5. *2 ripe tomatoes, crushed*

6. *1 tablespoon garlic/ginger paste, or 4 garlic cloves, mashed, and a piece fresh ginger, size of a walnut, minced*

NOTE: Garlic/ginger paste is so often used, and so convenient, that if you intend to do Indian cooking once a week or so, it is useful to make up garlic/ginger paste in quantity (see p. 23) and use it by the spoonful as needed.

7. *Full Masala:*

3-inch cinnamon stick, broken into pieces (8 cm)
4 cloves
2 black cardamom pods, crushed
2 green cardamom pods, crushed
1 teaspoon dried chili pepper flakes (equal to 2 dried pods)
1/2 teaspoon cumin seeds
1/2 teaspoon coriander seeds
2 bay leaves, crumbled

NOTE: If black cardamom is hard to find, use all green pods and double the amount called for. *Full Masala* always indicates the use of whole spices. These may be pushed aside by the diner, but they should remain in the dish when served. By altering quantities or even substituting spices, a cook can add his own signature to a full masala.

8. *Salt and freshly ground pepper to taste*
NOTE: Because of the flavors of the spices, salt can easily be cut down or even eliminated in many dishes. Black peppercorns are always to be ground fresh for each recipe.

9. *Dry masala:*

1 teaspoon turmeric
1/2 teaspoon ground coriander
1/2 teaspoon ground cumin
1/2 teaspoon paprika
1/4 teaspoon red chili powder

NOTE: The dry masala, which is added after *bhoona*-ing, often echoes the full masala, but in powder form the whole spices enter the meat during the first stage of cooking; the dry masala adds flavor to the sauce. Again, inventive cooks vary the ingredients of the dry masala according to personal style.

10. 1/2 cup yoghurt

11. 1 rounded teaspoon garam masala
NOTE: Garam masala is what Westerners call curry powder. In Indian stores, there are several different types of commercially prepared masalas. These are excellent for sprinkling over a completed vegetable or meat dish just prior to serving, as is chat masala in this recipe, but again this is a matter of personal taste.

12. 2 tablespoons chopped coriander leaves for garnish
NOTE: Many chefs, including those at the Bombay Palace kitchens, like to add a touch of bright green corinader leaves to garnish almost every dish and to add their own interesting taste. Chopped parsley can be substituted for color, but the effect will not be the same.

SUMMARY OF INGREDIENTS

SERVES 4-6

2 pounds baby lamb, all fat removed, boned, and cut into 2-inch cubes (1 kg in 5-cm cubes)
2 potatoes, peeled, each cut into 4 pieces
1/2 cup oil
2 medium onions, cut into thin half-rings
2 ripe tomatoes, crushed
1 tablespoon garlic/ginger paste

Full masala
Salt and fresh-ground pepper to taste
Dry masala
1/2 cup water
1/2 cup yoghurt
1 rounded teaspoon garam masala
2 tablespoons chopped coriander leaves for garnish

METHOD:
1. Prepare lamb and set aside.

2. Drop potatoes into boiling water and boil 5 minutes. Drain and set aside.

3. In a wok or heavy skillet heat the oil and saute the onions until they begin to turn dark brown.

> NOTE: Indian cooking often requires onions to be cooked until they are very dark brown, caramelized but never scorched. Constant stirring is necessary to produce browned onions that are the fullest in flavor.

4. Add the tomatoes, garlic/ginger paste, and the full masala. *Bhoona*, stirring frequently, until mixture becomes a paste. (NOTE: See notes on *bhoona*-ing, p. 13).

5. Add the lamb cubes and stir gently for 2 minutes, then add the dry masala. Add ½ cup water and *bhoona* for 20 minutes, being careful not to let the mixture scorch. If mixture gets too dry, add a spoonful of water from time to time.

6. Stir in the yoghurt and simmer for 5 minutes. Add about ½ cup water (depending on how thick you prefer your gravy) and then the boiled potatoes. Cover, and simmer until meat becomes tender, about 20 minutes.

7. Sprinkle the garam masala over the top, garnish with coriander leaves and serve.

> NOTE: To see this recipe in more condensed form, see Rogan Gosht, p. 88.

Chapter 5

APPETIZERS
and SOUPS

Indian appetizers are delightful to munch on at any time, whether as a prelude to a meal or along with cocktails. While many of the recipes here are served at the Bombay Palaces, you will find that with a bit of imagination you can make up various fillings to suit your own taste. You will find that these tidbits also go well as appetizers to precede an otherwise all Western menu.

While soups are not generally considered a part of traditional Indian dining, some Bombay Palace customers would not think of beginning a meal without this course. It is interesting to note that Mulligatawny transcended its Indian origin long ago and appears on menus everywhere in the world.

Mulligatawny Moghlai
MULLIGATAWNY SOUP

The original name of this soup in the Tamil language means "pepper water." Mulligatawny is such a popular soup that there are almost as many variations as there are Indian cooks. The Bombay Palace version is a bit more elegant than most.

SERVES 8-12.

2 pounds (1 kg) chicken bones,
   with all fat removed
1 whole chicken breast,
   boned, with all skin and fat
   removed
1/2 cup oil
4 garlic cloves, mashed
1 rounded tablespoon
   powdered ginger
1 large onion, chopped
1/2 pound (250 gm) besan
   (chick-pea flour)
4 ounces (120 gm) masoor dal
   (red lentils), cleaned well
8 cups water
2 teaspoons sugar

2 ounces (60 ml) milk
1 ounce (30 ml) heavy cream

Dry Masala:
1 teaspoon tamarind powder
   (2 teaspoons fresh lemon
   juice may be substituted)
1/2 teaspoon ground coriander
1/2 teaspoon ground cumin
1 teaspoon salt

Garnish:
The cooked chicken breast,
   julienned
3/4 cup steamed rice
small handful dry mint leaves

1. Prepare the chicken bones and the breast, making sure to remove absolutely all skin and fat. Set aside.

2. In a large soup pot heat the oil over medium heat. Add the garlic and the ginger, stirring constantly until the mixture turns golden, 3 to 5 minutes. Do not scorch. Add the onion and stir until it becomes translucent, about 8 minutes. Add the chicken bones (not the breast meat) and *bhoona* for 5 minutes, until bones take on color.

3. Lower heat and add the lentils and the besan flour. Stir constantly for 5 minutes. Add the dry masala and *bhoona* for 2 minutes.

4. Add 8 cups of water. Add the chicken breast, and bring mixture to boil. Stir gently now and then for 15 minutes.

5. Remove the breast meat. Partly cover the broth pot and simmer for 1 hour. Meanwhile, when the chicken breast is cool, slice it into thin slivers and set aside for garnish.

6. Strain the broth, pressing to extract as much liquid as possible. Discard bones and vegetables. Add the sugar, the milk and heavy cream. Reheat to just below boiling point.

7. Garnish each bowl with 3 or 4 slivers of the julienned chicken and 1 teaspoon of cooked rice. Top each bowl with a pinch of mint leaves.

Gobhi Shorba
CAULIFLOWER SOUP

SERVES 6.

2 cups water
1 quart (1 liter) milk
1/2 pound (1/4 kg) cauliflower
   flowerets, cut into 1 1/2-inch
   (4 cm) cubes
2 ounces (60 gms) cashews,
   chopped fine

1 teaspoon sugar
1 teaspoon salt
1/2 teaspoon (8 gm) butter
freshly ground pepper, to taste
coriander leaves for garnish

1. In a soup pot heat the milk, cauliflower, cashews, and water over a medium flame. Stir gently every 3 minutes for 20 minutes. Let cool.

2. Puree the mixture in a blender or food processor.

3. Return the soup to the pot. Add the sugar, salt and pepper. When soup nears the boiling point, gently stir in the butter, and serve immediately.

4. Garnish each bowl with a few coriander leaves.

Murgh Shorba
CHICKEN SOUP PUNJABI STYLE

SERVES 4-6.

4 ounces (120 gm) butter (1
  stick)
1/2 cup flour
2 tablespoons garlic/ginger
  paste or
    6 small garlic cloves,
      mashed
    piece of fresh ginger size of a
      Brazil nut, minced

Dry Masala:
1/2 teaspoon cinnamon powder
1/2 teaspoon cardamom
powder
1/2 teaspoon ground coriander

1/2 teaspoon paprika
1/2 teaspoon turmeric
1/2 teaspoon garam masala
1/2 teaspoon red chili powder

2 quarts (2 liters) chicken
  stock (see note below)
1 breast of chicken, skinned
  and boned, then minced
  (meat can be precooked)
1 teaspoon sugar
1 teaspoon salt
1/2 cup milk

1/4 cup heavy cream
freshly ground pepper to taste

NOTE: If you are making stock from scratch, bring 2 pounds
of chicken bones to boil in 3 quarts of water (2 1/2 liters). Skim
off surface scum, and reduce to 2 quarts. This will take about
1 hour.

1. In a large soup pot, melt the butter over medium heat. Sprinkle in the flour and stir steadily until the mixture just begins to turn golden brown.

2. Stir in the garlic/ginger paste and the dry masala, blending well.

3. Add the stock.

4. Bring soup to the boil, then lower heat and simmer 10 minutes.

5. Add the minced chicken breast, the sugar and salt, and the 1/2 cup of milk. Simmer 5 minutes.

When serving, top with a teaspoon of heavy cream in the center of each bowl. Grind a bit of black pepper in the center of the cream.

Gosht
MEAT SOUP

SERVES 4.

1 pound (¹/₂ kg) meat (beef
    preferred, but lamb may be
    used)
4 cups water
1 large onion, chopped
1 rounded tablespoon
    garlic/ginger paste or
    3 garlic cloves, mashed
    1 piece fresh ginger, size of
    walnut, minced

1¹/₂ teaspoons salt
4 ripe tomatoes, peeled and
    quartered
2 ounces (60 gm) noodles
    (optional)
2 tablespoons chopped
    coriander leaves for garnish
generous grinding of black
    pepper

1. Cut meat into 1-inch (3-cm) cubes and place in a wok or heavy saucepan with the water, onion, garlic/ginger paste, salt, pepper and tomatoes, and bring to a boil. Remove scum that rises until the broth is clear. Simmer, partially covered, for 1 hour.

2. Strain the soup through a sieve, and return meat to the saucepan. Press remaining solids to extract as much liquid as possible and discard. Add the noodles to the soup. Return the pot to the stove and simmer until noodles are done, about 7 minutes. Garnish each bowl with coriander leaves and serve hot.

Kaddu
PUMPKIN SOUP

SERVES 4.

1 pound fresh pumpkin, peeled
  and cut into 1-inch (3 cm)
  cubes
1 large ripe tomato, peeled
  and quartered
1 large potato, peeled and
  quartered
1¹/₂ cups chicken broth (or
  water)

1 teaspoon salt
generous grinding of black
  pepper
1 piece fresh ginger, size of
  almond, minced.
4 tablespoons yoghurt for
  garnish

1. In a wok or heavy saucepan put the pumpkin, tomato, potato and the stock and bring to a boil. Lower heat to medium and simmer for 25 minutes or until vegetables are tender. Season with salt and pepper, and add the ginger.

2. Remove pot from heat, scoop out the vegetables with a slotted spoon and put them a blender to puree them. Sieve the puree to make it finer, or return it to the pot as it is. Garnish each bowl with a spoonful of yoghurt and serve hot.

Gobhi Pakoras
CAULIFLOWER FRITTERS

MAKES 12-15 FRITTERS.

Batter:
1 cup chick-pea flour (besan)
1/2 cup flour
1/2 teaspoon baking powder
1/2 teaspoon red chili flakes
1/2 teaspoon salt
1/4 teaspoon cumin seeds
1/4 teaspoon paprika
1/4 teaspoon ground turmeric
1/4 teaspoon sugar

1 tablespoon oil
1 large head cauliflower
oil for deep frying (about 1
   cup)

1. Combine the flours, baking powder, spices and sugar in a large bowl. Add the tablespoon of oil and beat with electric beater for 2 minutes, until batter is smooth and creamy.

2. Wash cauliflower and divide into flowerets. Cook in boiling water for 5 minutes. Drain and cool.

3. In a wok or skillet heat the oil, just to the smoking point (about 375°F). Using tongs, dip one floweret at a time into the batter and then into the hot oil. Fry the flowerets in batches of 5 pieces until golden, or about 5 minutes. As they brown, remove and drain on paper towels. Keep warm.

NOTE: This same method can be used to make eggplant fritters.

Chana
CHICK-PEA APPETIZER

SERVES 6-8.

1 pound chick-peas, or 2
   1-pound (1/2 kg) cans cooked
   chick-peas
2 tablespoons oil
1 onion, minced

1 teaspoon red chili powder
1/2 teaspoon salt
generous grinding of black
   pepper
juice of 1 lemon

1. Sort and wash chick-peas. Soak for 4 hours in plenty of water. Bring to boil in fresh water. Cover and simmer until tender, about 1 hour. Stir occasionally, but gently so as not to break the peas. Drain and cool. Drain liquid and save for another use.
NOTE: If using canned chick-peas, skip this step.

2. In a wok or heavy skillet heat the oil and saute the minced onion until translucent. Add all the other ingredients, the lemon juice last, and heat through. Serve hot as a vegetable dish, or cool and serve as an appetizer or part of a salad.

3. Garnish with tardka (p. 25) if desired.

Tooka
INDIAN FRIED POTATOES

SERVES 4.

2 large potatoes, peeled and
   cut into rounds 1/2 inch (11/2
   cm) thick
1/2 cup peanut oil

1/2 teaspoon red chili flakes
1/2 teaspoon ground coriander
1/2 teaspoon ground cumin
salt to taste

In a wok or heavy skillet, heat oil just to smoking point. Fry the potatoes in the hot oil. When about half-done, remove and press each slice to half its thickness. Return the slices to the hot oil, add all of the spices, and fry until golden brown. Serve them piping hot.

Piaz Pakoras
ONION FRITTERS

SERVES 4-6.

1 cup chick-pea flour (besan)
2 teaspoons vegetable oil
2 green chilies, minced
1 teaspoon salt
1 teaspoon ground cumin

1/2 cup warm water
2 onions sliced in paper-thin
    rings
oil for deep frying, about 1 cup

1. Sift the flour into a large bowl. Add 2 teaspoons of vegetable oil and rub mixture with your fingers to make a crumbly mass. Work in chilies, salt and cumin. Slowly add 1/2 cup of warm water (about 100° F), constantly stirring the mixture with a wire whisk until you get a smooth, thick batter. You can also make the batter in a blender.

2. Using an electric beater, beat the batter until it turns light and fluffy, about 10 minutes. Cover, and let rest in warm place (such as an oven with a pilot light on) for 1/2 hour. The batter will become very spongy.

3. Prepare the onion rings and add them to the batter when it is ready.

4. In a wok or heavy skillet heat the oil just to the smoking point (about 375°F). Using a large spoon, drop in 2 or 3 tablespoonsful of the onion mixture to make each fritter, filling the pan with about 5 fritters at a time. Keep the oil temperature constant by regulating the flame, so that the fritters turn golden all over. Remove with a slotted spoon, drain on paper towels, and keep warm.

5. Repeat with the rest of the mixture.

Chicken Pakoras
CHICKEN FRITTERS

SERVES 6.

1 3-pound (1 1/2 kg) chicken,
  boned, skinned and cut into
  finger-size strips

Pakora Dough:
1/4 pound (125 gm) besan
  (chick-pea flour)
2 ounces (60 gm) white flour
2 eggs

1 teaspoon salt
1/2 teaspoon fresh-ground
  pepper
1/4 teaspoon red pepper powder
1/4 teaspoon baking powder
1 teaspoon egg color (optional)
2 teaspoons lemon juice

oil for deep frying

1. In a bowl put all ingredients and add enough water to make a batter as thick as ketchup. Add the chicken strips and coat well with the batter.

2. In a wok or heavy skillet pour oil to depth of about 2 inches (5 cm) and heat to 375°F.

3. Using tongs, drop the strips of chicken into the hot oil and deep-fry until golden brown, about 5 minutes. Serve while hot.

Assorted Pakoras

Pakoras are similar to samosas except that the dough is made differently. Both make excellent snacks, and appetizers for the cocktail hour, as well as being good as side dishes with a meal.

Pastry:
1/4 pound (120 gm) besan
   (chick-pea flour)
1/4 teaspoon each of:
   cumin seed
   salt
   red chili powder
   baking powder
1/2 teaspoon egg color
   (optional)
1/2 cup water
oil for deep frying

Cauliflower Filling:
1/2 head cauliflower, with core
   removed, shredded and
   seasoned lightly with salt

Potato Filling:
1 large potato, boiled and
   peeled and diced

(Cashew nuts and raisins, fresh green peas or other vegetable or meat mixtures of your choice [such as keema] can also be used as fillings.)

1. In a bowl mix all ingredients with about 1/2 cup of water, to make a soft dough (like a cookie dough).

2. To form the pakoras, take a rounded teaspoon of dough and roll it into a small circle. Pick up the dough and roll it into a cone in your hand. Put about a teaspoon of the filling into the cone and press the top over to seal the cone well. Press gently into a triangular shape.

3. In a wok or heavy skillet, pour oil to the depth of 2 inches (6 cm) and heat to 375°. Deep-fry the pakoras, pressing gently with a spatula to brown on all sides. When golden, remove pakoras and drain on paper towels. Serve while hot.

Sabzi Bora
VEGETABLE CROQUETTES

MAKES ABOUT 40 CROQUETTES.

2 pounds (1 kg) carrots,
  cooked and mashed
12 ounces (¹/₂ kg) green peas,
  cooked and mashed (or one
  pack frozen)
1¹/₄ cups puffed rice cereal,
  ground to fine crumbs
3 tablespoons (45 gm) butter
2 green chilies, seeded and
  chopped
¹/₄ cup light cream

¹/₂ teaspoon ground roasted
  cumin, roasted in a pan for
  6 seconds
¹/₂ teaspon cumin seeds
¹/₂ teaspoon garam masala
  (see pp. 15–19)
1 teaspoon salt
2 eggs, separated into yolks
  and whites
6 ounces seasoned bread
  crumbs

1. Combine all ingredients except the egg whites and bread crumbs.

2. Beat the egg whites until stiff and gently fold into the vegetable mixture. Cover and chill for 2 hours.

3. Grease a shallow baking pan. Shape the vegetable mixture into 1-inch (3-cm) balls.

4. Put the seasoned crumbs into a plastic bag and, adding a few of the croquettes at a time, shake until they are evenly coated with crumbs. Place on the baking pan and chill ¹/₂ hour or until ready to bake.

5. Preheat oven to 400° F. Bake the croquettes for 12 minutes or until golden. OR: Deep-fry the chilled croquettes in hot oil (375° F) about 5-7 minutes until golden and crisp. Drain on paper towels. Serve at once.

Keema Samosa
SPICY MEAT PATTIES

MAKES ABOUT 30 PATTIES.

1 recipe keema (see pp. 65–66; 99–102)

Samosa Dough:
1½ cups all-purpose flour
½ teaspoon salt

3 tablespoons sweet butter
½ cup water, approximately

oil to cover bottom of a wok or skillet to a depth of 3 inches (8 cm)

1. In a mixing bowl, put flour and salt. Add butter. Adding water a spoonful at a time, mix with fingers to form a soft dough. Let rest ½ hour.

2. When you are ready to make the patties, knead the dough a few minutes, then divide it into 2 equal portions. With your hands, roll each portion into a rope ½ inch thick (1½ cm). Cut the ropes into 8 parts, and roll the small pieces of dough into balls.

3. When you have made all the balls, take each one and put it on a lightly floured board. Roll it into a 5-inch (12 cm) circle. Cut the circle in half. Each half makes one patty.

4. Moisten the straight edge of a semicircle with water, then overlap the dry side onto the moist side in order to make a cone. Press edges well to make a seal.

5. Put 1 tablespoon ground meat into the cone. Moisten the open end of the cone and pinch shut, forming a fat triangle. Be sure each cone is well sealed so it won't come apart during frying.

6. When all the cones have been filled and sealed, heat the oil in the wok or skillet until hot (350° F). Drop in enough pastries to fill the pan, about 6. Keep the oil temperature constant so the patties will brown slowly. This will keep them flaky. When they are lightly golden (about 10 minutes), remove with tongs and drain on paper towels.

7. Serve as main dish, or as a side dish with chutneys or coriander-mint sauce (see p. 181).

Bhujias
ONION FRITTERS

These are wonderful as appetizers and equally wonderful to serve with cocktails.

MAKES ABOUT 15 BHUJIAS.

1 large onion, chopped fine
2 fresh green chilies, chopped
   fine
$^1/_4$ cup methi (fenugreek)
   leaves; or substitute celery
   leaves (use the tips from the
   inner stalks only)
3 tablespoons chopped
   coriander leaves

$^1/_4$ teaspoon each of:
   cumin seeds
   red chili powder
   turmeric
   salt
   sugar
4 tablespoons besan
   (chick-pea flour)
oil for deep frying

1. In a bowl combine all the ingredients except the oil and mix well with just enough water to make a sticky dough.

2. In a wok or heavy skillet, heat the oil to 375°F. Use two teaspoons, one to scoop up a bit of dough and the other to shape it into a small ball. Scrape the dough ball into the hot oil and fry, pressing lightly with a spatula to crisp balls on all sides. When the bhujias turn golden, in about 5 minutes, remove and drain on paper towels. Serve while hot.

Samosas
FILLED TURNOVERS

Samosas are very similar to pakoras, except that the dough is made differently. The fillings can be the same. Like pakoras, samosas make good appetizers and excellent snacks for the cocktail hour, as well as being good served with a meal as a side dish.

SERVES 4-6.

Pastry:
1 pound (¹/₂ kg) unbleached
  white flour
2 tablespoons chopped
  coriander leaves
2¹/₂ tablespoons oil
¹/₄ teaspoon cumin seed,
  toasted
¹/₄ teaspoon red chili powder

Fillings:
(see Fillings for Pakora, p. 57)

oil for deep frying

1. In a bowl mix all the ingredients except the cooking oil, first toasting the cumin seeds a few moments in a dry skillet until they begin to hop about. Add a bit of water to make a fairly stiff dough. Knead about 10 minutes. Cut off pieces of the dough and roll between your palms to make "golf balls". Let the dough balls rest for 15 minutes.

2. On a work surface, sprinkle a thin layer of flour, and roll out a ball of dough into a very thin oval, about 9 inches (23 cm) long. Cut the oval in half to make two semicircles.

3. Use one of the fillings suggested for pakoras, or make up a meat or vegetable filling of your choice. Put a rounded teaspoon of the filling in the center of a semicircle, lightly wet the edges of the semicircle with water and carefully fold it over to make a triangle. Press the edges lightly to make a seal.

4. In a wok or heavy skillet, add 2 inches (5 cm) oil and heat to 375°. Drop in the samosas and press lightly with a spatula so that they become crisp all over. When golden brown, remove and drain on paper towels. Serve while hot.

Dosai #I
RICE PANCAKES

These delectable pancakes are a breakfast treat in Southern India, but are delicious anywhere at any time.

MAKES ABOUT 10 CAKES.

1 1/2 cups rice flour (obtainable in Indian shops and health-food stores)
1 1/2 cups unbleached white flour

3 tablespoons yoghurt
1 teaspoon salt
water

1. Sift the two flours into a bowl. Add the yoghurt and salt, and, using a wooden spoon, gradually beat in enough water to make a thick, smooth batter (about 2 1/2 cups).

2. Let the batter set overnight in a warm place (such as in an oven with a pilot light), or until it ferments.

3. Lightly grease a wok or heavy skillet. When the oil is hot, pour in just enough batter to make a pancake about the size of a saucer. Cook until underside becomes golden brown, then flip and cook half a minute on the other side.

4. Serve hot with fresh grated coconut or with chutneys.

Dosai #II
RICE PANCAKES

Because dosai are popular all over South India, and in other places, too, there are many neighborhood versions, as in the following recipe.

MAKES ABOUT 6 PANCAKES.

9 ounces cream of wheat or semolina (260 gm)
1 1/2 cups water
1 tablespoon sour milk, or buttermilk
1/2 teaspoon baking soda
1/4 teaspoon salt

NOTE: If desired, the dough can be spiced a bit by adding one small green chili, minced, 1 teaspoon fenugreek (methi), and 1 teaspoon sugar.

butter for frying pancakes

60

Put all ingredients in a bowl and beat well with a wooden spoon until creamy. Let the mixture set overnight in a warm place (such as an oven with a pilot light), until it ferments.

Meanwhile make a filling—as for pakoras or samosas, or try this special one:

SPECIAL DOSAI FILLING

2 potatoes, boiled, peeled and
  diced
2 onions, minced
2 green chilies, minced
1/2 teaspoon salt

1/2 teaspoon mustard seeds
1/4 teaspoon turmeric
1/4 teaspoon garlic/ginger paste
  (optional)
1 tablespoon oil

1. Prepare the potatoes.

2. In a wok or heavy skillet, heat 1 tablespoon oil and add the mustard seeds. When they stop sputtering, add the onions and the green chilies and stir-fry until onions are translucent. Add the rest of the spices and stir a few seconds. Then add the diced potatoes. Blend well.

NOTE: At this point, if you want, you can add any leftover keema, dal, or any kind of chopped meat, if desired, along with a bit of chopped tomato, a little fried onion, or anything your imagination suggests.

TO COOK THE DOSAI: Butter the bottom of a wok or heavy skillet with 2 or 3 tablespoons of butter. When the butter is sizzling, pour in enough batter to make a circle the size of a saucer. Cover with a lid and cook for about 2 minutes until the cake has "set." Remove the lid and put a rounded teaspoon of filling in the center. Fold the cake over like an omelet, and if necessary add a bit more butter to brown the cake.

Serve hot, with fresh grated coconut or chutneys.

Chuza Chat
SPICY CHICKEN SALAD

This delightfully piquant dish can be served either as an appetizer or as a main dish, depending on the quantity made.

SERVES 4 AS A MAIN DISH;

SERVES 6 OR MORE AS AN APPETIZER OR SALAD.

1 3-pound chicken, boiled, skinned and boned, then cut into small cubes (1½ kg)
1 onion, chopped fine
1 tablespoon dry masala (p. 15)
1 tablespoon chopped coriander leaves

generous grinding of black pepper
½ teaspoon salt
juice of half a large lemon
1 tablespoon tomato puree (or canned tomato sauce)
1 tablespoon cumin seeds

1. Prepare chicken (p. 37). When cool, cut into small cubes. Set aside.

2. Chop the onion and mix it in a bowl with the rest of the ingredients—except for the cumin seeds.

3. In a small fry pan toast the cumin seeds over low heat until they begin to turn golden and hop about. Do not scorch. Lightly crush the cumin seeds and mix them with the other ingredients. Add the chicken and blend gently.

4. Chill for a few hours or overnight. Serve each portion on a bed of crisp lettuce leaves.

Chicken Chat

This delightful, piquant dish can be served either as an appetizer or as a main dish, depending on the quantity made.

SERVES 4 AS MAIN DISH;
SERVES 6 AS AN APPETIZER.

1 3-pound chicken, boiled,
    skinned, boned and diced
    (1¹/₂ kg) (pp. 8, 37)
1 potato, boiled, peeled, and
    diced
2 tomatoes
1 cup yoghurt
1 teaspoon sugar

¹/₂ teaspoon each:
    red pepper powder
    fresh-ground black pepper
¹/₄ teaspoon salt
juice of ¹/₂ lemon
1 teaspoon cumin seed,
    toasted
lettuce leaves and 2
    tablespoons chopped
    coriander leaves for garnish

1. Prepare the chicken. Set aside.

2. When ready to prepare the dish, boil and then dice the potato. Set aside. Cut one tomato into small cubes and the other into thin slices. Set the sliced tomato rings aside.

3. Make a salad by mixing well all the ingredients except the tomato rings, the cumin seeds and the lettuce leaves.

4. In a small fry pan toast the cumin seeds for ¹/₂ minute, until they begin to dance and change color. Sprinkle the seeds over the salad.

5. Arrange the lettuce leaves on a plate, and spread the chicken salad in the center. Garnish by placing the tomato rings around the edge of the salad. Sprinkle coriander leaves on top.

Chapter 6

POULTRY SPECIALTIES

In India, as in many lands, chicken is a favorite ingredient for a wide variety of dishes. Chicken is so versatile that it can be substituted for almost any other meat except beef. Reversing the procedure will not work: Many chicken dishes are so delicately spiced that substituting a stronger meat would adversely affect the recipe.

Duck is not commonly used in the Indian cuisines, except in Portuguese-influenced Goa. Oddly enough, the incendiary vindaloo, another culinary triumph for Goa, is also attributed to the early Portuguese traders and settlers there, rather than to the indigenous Indians.

Murgh Keema Masala
MINCED CHICKEN "DRY CURRY"

SERVES 4-6.

2 pounds (1 kg) boneless
   chicken, skinned, then
   ground
2 ounces (60 gm) cashew nuts,
   ground to a paste
1/4 cup oil

Full Masala:
1 3-inch (8 cm) piece
   cinnamon
4 cloves
2 green cardamom pods,
   crushed
1/2 teaspoon cumin seeds

3 medium onions, chopped
   fine

Dry Masala:
1/2 teaspoon ground coriander
1/2 teaspoon ground cumin
1/2 teaspoon ground turmeric

1/4 teaspoon red chili powder
1/4 teaspoon paprika

1/4 teaspoon salt
generous grinding of black
   pepper

3 tomatoes, chopped fine
1 tablespoon garlic/ginger
   paste or
   3 cloves garlic, mashed
   1 piece fresh ginger, size of
    walnut, minced
1/2 cup yoghurt

2 ounces cashews (60 gm),
   ground to paste
4 tablespoons heavy cream
1 1/2 cups fresh peas (or
   substitute 1 package frozen)
2 tablespoons chopped
   coriander leaves for garnish

1. Prepare chicken by grinding in food processor or putting through fine blade of meat grinder. Set aside. Grind cashews to a paste in a mortar or use a blender, adding a bit of water. Set aside.

2. In a wok or heavy skillet heat the oil and add the full masala, and *bhoona* for 1/2 minute. Add the onions and the dry masala. Stir. Add the chicken and *bhoona* 2 minutes.

3. Add the tomatoes and the garlic/ginger paste and *bhoona* 5 minutes to dry the mixture. Stir constantly to avoid scorching. Add 1/2 cup water and simmer 5 minutes, until mixture

again becomes dry. (See p. 13.)

4. Add yoghurt and *bhoona* 2 minutes. Add the cashew paste and *bhoona* 1/2 minute. Add 1/2 cup water, and simmer 5 minutes. Add the cream and mix well. Add the peas, mix well, and simmer 5 more minutes, until peas are barely cooked and mixture is dry.
NOTE: Traditionally the murgh keema masala should be dry. If you like a little gravy, add a little water, about 1/2 cup or so, when you add the peas.

5. Garnish with coriander leaves.

Keema Masala
DRY-COOKED LAMB OR BEEF

Using the same recipe as for chicken, lamb or beef may be substituted. If so, you can add 3 medium potatoes, peeled and sliced into quarters, at the end of step 3. In addition, add 1 1/2 cups water and cook long enough to make the potatoes tender. Further, as the keema finishes cooking, you can also add 4 hardboiled eggs, sliced in half lengthwise, when you add the peas. There should be enough gravy to coat the eggs.

Indian Missny
CHICKEN GREEN PEPPER CURRY

SERVES 4.

1 3-pound (1 1/2 kg) chicken, skinned and cut into 8 parts
2 teaspoons black peppercorns, crushed
1/2 teaspoon turmeric
1/2 teaspoon salt
2 large onions, sliced into paper-thin rings

4 tablespoons oil
1/2 green pepper, minced (use either bell or chili pepper as desired)
1 cup thick coconut milk (p. 35)
1 cup fresh green peas (or 1 package frozen)

1. Prepare chicken. Combine the peppercorns, turmeric and salt. Rub well into chicken parts and set aside.

2. In a wok or heavy skillet, heat the oil over high heat and saute the onion rings until they turn golden brown. Add the chicken and the green pepper. *Bhoona* 5 minutes. Add 1/2 cup water, cover, and simmer 20 minutes. (For *bhoona* technique, see p. 13.)

3. Add the coconut milk, mixing well. Simmer, uncovered, until chicken is tender, about 10 minutes. Stir in the green peas, simmer 3 minutes, and serve.

Palace Murgh Kari
BOMBAY PALACE CHICKEN CURRY

(Note: Detailed commentary on preparing this dish can be found in the Master Demonstration recipe on page 36.)

SERVES 4.

1 3-pound (1 1/2 kg) fryer, skinned and cut into 8 pieces
3 tomatoes, diced

Full Masala:
3 pieces cinnamon stick, 1 inch (3 cm) long
4 black cardamom pods, crushed
6 green cardamom pods, crushed
6 cloves
1/2 teaspoon cumin seeds, crushed
2 dried red peppers, crushed, or substitute 1 teaspoon dried pepper flakes

1/4 cup oil
3 onions, chopped fine
1 teaspoon garlic/ginger paste
salt and fresh-ground pepper to taste

Dry Masala:
1 teaspoon cumin powder
1 1/2 teaspoons coriander powder
1 teaspoon turmeric
1 tablespoon garam masala
1/2 teaspoon red chili powder

1/2 cup yoghurt
1 rounded tablespoon tomato paste
4 tablespoons heavy cream
2 tablespoons coriander leaves, for garnish

1. Prepare the chicken and set aside.

2. Dice tomatoes, set aside.

3. In a wok or heavy skillet, heat the oil and add the full masala. *Bhoona* for 1/2 minute, add the onions and stir-fry until they turn golden.

4. Add the garlic/ginger paste, and the dry masala. *Bhoona* the mixture over medium-high heat, adding 1/2 cup water if necessary to prevent scorching.

5. Add the chicken and tomatoes, stirring constantly for 5 minutes. Add the yoghurt, reduce heat and *bhoona* for 10-15 minutes while the chicken absorbs the spices. During this time, if sauce gets too dry, or if you prefer plenty of gravy, add 1/2 cup water. Finally, stir in the tomato paste and the heavy cream.

6. Garnish with the coriander leaves and serve.

Murgh Do Piaza
CHICKEN IN MILD CURRY TOPPED WITH ONIONS AND TOMATOES

This is similar to the basic Bombay Chicken Curry recipe. *Do Piaza* translates as "with two onions", but you see that 3 onions are used, prepared in two different ways. Lamb and beef are also widely used as a basis for Do Piaza dishes (see p. 90).

SERVES 4-6.

1 3½-pound (1½ kg) chicken, skinned and cut into 8 serving pieces (deboned if preferred)
3 tablespoons (45 gm) butter
1 large onion, chopped fine
1 garlic clove, crushed

Dry Masala:
½ teaspoon ground cardamom

¼ teaspoon ground cinnamon
¼ teaspoon red chili powder
¼ teaspoon turmeric
1 bay leaf

2 cups chicken stock
2 large onions, sliced in paper-thin rings (see NOTE*)*
1 tablespoon oil
3 tablespoons heavy cream
salt to taste

NOTE: For all Do Piaza dishes, onions should be cut in half vertically, then sliced into thin half-rings. For such dishes, a quartered tomato is also often added as part of the garnish.

1. Prepare chicken and set aside.

2. In a wok or heavy skillet melt half the butter and brown the chicken well on all sides. Remove from pan and keep warm.

3. Heat remaining butter in the pan, add the onion and garlic and saute until onion begins to brown. Do not scorch. Stir in the dry masala and continue cooking for 3 minutes. Gradually add the stock. Bring mixture to a boil, stir, simmer for 20 minutes.

4. While the gravy simmers, in a separate small skillet heat the oil and add the onion rings. Over high heat, stir gently but constantly until the onions begin to caramelize. Set aside.

5. Return the chicken to the sauce, cover and simmer for 30 minutes, or until tender. Stir in the heavy cream. Salt to taste. Top with the fried onion rings and serve.

Murgh Masala
SPICY CHICKEN CURRY

1 3-pound (1¹/₂ kg) fryer,
  skinned and cut into eight
  pieces

Dry Masala:
1 large onion, coarsely
  chopped
1 tablespoon garlic/ginger
  paste, or:
  3 cloves garlic, mashed
  1 piece fresh ginger, size of
    walnut, minced
2 tablespoons ground
  coriander

2 teaspoons cumin seeds
2 teaspoons powdered
  turmeric
¹/₄ teaspoon red chili powder
6 cloves
3 whole cardamom pods
2 sticks of cinnamon

4 tablespoons (60 gm) butter
  (¹/₂ stick)
4 large ripe tomatoes, coarsely
  chopped
salt to taste

1. Prepare chicken and set aside. In a blender or food processor pulverize the dry masala. Rub the masala well into the chicken parts.

2. In a wok or heavy skillet, heat the butter and brown the chicken on both sides. This should take about 10 minutes. Add the tomatoes, cover and simmer until chicken is tender and the sauce has thickened, about 10 minutes. Do not add water unless the chicken threatens to scorch. Salt the dish lightly before serving.

Murgh Vindaloo
CHICKEN VINDALOO

Vindaloos, the extra-spicy-hot dishes from Portuguese Goa, are most often made with pork, sometimes duck. However, any meat can be done in a vindaloo sauce, as in this recipe.

SERVES 4.

1 3-pound (1¹/₂ kg) chicken,
  skinned and chopped into 8
  pieces (deboned if preferred)

Marinade:
1 cup yoghurt
¹/₄ cup white vinegar
2 tablespoons garlic/ginger
  paste, or:
  6 garlic cloves, mashed
  1 piece fresh ginger, size of a
    Brazil nut, minced

2 onions, chopped fine
2 tomatoes, chopped fine
2 tablespoons oil

Dry Masala:
1 teaspoon dried red pepper
  flakes
¹/₄ teaspoon turmeric
¹/₄ teaspoon paprika

1 large potato, peeled and
  cubed
1 tablespoon tomato paste
salt and freshly ground pepper
  to taste
2 tablespoons coriander leaves
  for garnish

1. Prepare chicken and set aside.

2. Make marinade and add chicken pieces. Mix well and marinate at least 4 hours and preferably overnight.

3. In a wok or heavy skillet, heat the oil and saute the onions until they begin to turn brown. Add tomatoes and the dry masala. *Bhoona* over high heat, stirring constantly, for 5 min-utes. Add the meat and its marinade. Simmer 20 minutes. Add the cubed potato, the tomato paste and about ¹/₂ cup water (or more if you prefer more gravy). Cover, and simmer for 10 min-utes, or until chicken and potatoes are tender.

4. Garnish with coriander leaves and serve.

Murgh Makhani
BUTTER CHICKEN

This is a classic Punjabi dish. Rich, velvety and delectable, with just enough spice to tantalize the palate, the Bombay Palace version is unequalled. Traditionally, the dish is made from Tandoori Chicken, and you should always make enough of that recipe to allow for ample leftovers. However, you can also make the dish from scratch, using the following recipe. The fragrant coriander leaves are an essential ingredient; without this garnish the Butter Chicken will be short of perfection.

1 3-pound (1¹/₂ kg) chicken, skinned, boned, and cut into 8 pieces; or, 3 pounds leftover tandoori chicken
1 tablespoon garlic/ginger paste or
3 garlic cloves, mashed
1 piece of fresh ginger, size of walnut, minced
juice 1 lemon

Sauce:
2 pounds tomatoes, seeded and pulped
4 ounces (120 gm) butter (1 stick)
¹/₂ teaspoon salt
generous grinding of pepper
6 ounces (180 ml) heavy cream
1 green chili, julienned

2 tablespoons chopped coriander leaves for garnish

1. If you have leftover tandoori chicken, bone and cut into small chunks, and go on to step 3. Otherwise begin from scratch. Prepare chicken pieces and rub with garlic/ginger paste and lemon juice. Marinate at least 10 hours or overnight.

2. Preheat oven to 500° F at least ¹/₂ hour before using. Set the chicken pieces in a shallow pan and roast 15 minutes on the first side, about 10 on the second. *To grill:* brush grill with a bit of oil to prevent sticking. Place chicken pieces over extremely hot bed of coals, and grill for 15 minutes on one side, and another 10 minutes on the other. Baste once on each side.

3. In a wok or heavy skillet simmer the tomatoes gently until their liquid evaporates, leaving a thick paste. This will take 5-10 minutes. Add the butter, salt and pepper. Add the cream, the julienned chili, then the chicken pieces. Simmer gently 5 minutes.

4. Transfer the chicken to a heated serving dish, garnishing with the chopped coriander. Serve with rice or any Indian bread.

Murgh Saag
CHICKEN WITH SPINACH IN GRAVY

SERVES 4.

1 3-pound (1¹/₂ kg) chicken,
  skinned, boned and cut into
  8 pieces
1 pound fresh spinach (or 2
  packages frozen), cooked
  and chopped
¹/₄ cup oil

Full Masala:
1 3-inch (8 cm) cinnamon
  stick, broken in pieces
6 green cardamom pods,
  crushed
4 black cardamom pods,
  crushed (or use 12 green
  pods in all)
4 cloves
¹/₄ teaspoon cumin seeds

2 onions, diced
1 tablespoon garlic/ginger
  paste or
3 garlic cloves, mashed

1 piece fresh ginger, size of
  walnut, minced
2 tomatoes, diced

Dry Masala:
³/₄ teaspoon ground coriander
¹/₂ teaspoon ground cumin
¹/₂ teaspoon ground fenugreek
¹/₂ teaspoon ground paprika
¹/₂ teaspoon turmeric
¹/₄ teaspoon red chili powder
salt and freshly ground pepper
  to taste

4 tablespoons yoghurt
1 tablespoon cashews, ground
  with a bit of water to make
  a paste
4 tablespoons heavy cream
2 tablespoons chopped
  coriander leaves for garnish

1. Prepare chicken and set aside.

2. Squeeze dry spinach and stir-fry 1 minute in a scant tablespoon of oil. Set aside.

3. In a wok or heavy skillet heat the rest of the oil. Add the full masala and *bhoona* 1 minute. Add the onions and saute until golden brown. If necessary, add a sprinkle of water to keep the onions soft. (See p. 13 for *bhoona*.)

4. Add the garlic/ginger paste and the tomatoes. *Bhoona* 5 minutes, turning meat to brown evenly. Add the dry masala, the yoghurt, cashew paste and cream and *bhoona* 5 minutes, or until liquid becomes a thick paste. Add a sprinkle of water if necessary to avoid scorching. If chicken is not tender, again add a sprinkle of water, cover, and simmer about 5 minutes.

5. Turn heat to high, add the cooked spinach and stir-fry 2 minutes. Garnish with coriander and serve.

Murgh Jalfrasie
CHICKEN WITH MIXED VEGETABLES

SERVES 4.

1 3-pound (1¹/₂ kg) chicken,
  skinned, boned and cut into
  strips 2 inches x 1 inch (6
  cm x 3 cm)
4 tablespoons (60 gm) butter
  (¹/₂ stick)
1 teaspoon cumin seeds
2 onions, chopped
2 green bell peppers, seeded
  and cored, cut into 1-inch
  (3 cm) cubes
2 large tomatoes, coarsely
  chopped

Dry Masala:
¹/₂ teaspoon paprika

¹/₂ teaspoon red chili powder
¹/₂ teaspoon turmeric

1 tablespoon garlic/ginger
  paste or
  3 garlic cloves, mashed
  1 piece fresh ginger, size of a
    walnut, minced
2 tablespoons white vinegar
2 tablespoons tomato puree
¹/₄ cup chicken stock (water or
  dry white wine may be
  substituted)
2 tablespoons chopped
  coriander leaves
salt and fresh-ground pepper
  to taste

1. Prepare chicken and set aside.

2. In a wok or heavy skillet, melt the butter and add the cumin seeds. Saute gently for ¹/₂ minute until they begin to dance. Add the chicken, and when it turns white add the onions, peppers, and tomatoes. *Bhoona* for 4 minutes, until mixture becomes dry.

3. Add the dry masala, garlic/ginger paste, vinegar, tomato puree and the chicken stock. *Bhoona* over medium-high heat for 3-5 minutes, until sauce is reduced and the vegetables are cooked but still quite crunchy. Season with salt and pepper, as desired.

4. Garnish with coriander leaves and serve.

Talawa Murgh Hindustani
FRIED CHICKEN INDIAN STYLE

1 3-pound (1^1/$_2$ kg) chicken
  skinned and cut into 8
  pieces (pp. 8, 37)
^{1}/$_2$ teaspoon turmeric
Salt and freshly ground pepper
  to taste

Full Masala:
1 teaspoon garlic/ginger paste,
  or:
  1 clove garlic, mashed
  1 piece fresh ginger, size of
  almonds, minced
6 peppercorns

5 green cardamom pods,
  crushed
4 cloves
1 1-inch (3 cm) piece
  cinnamon
2 teaspoons coriander seeds
^{1}/$_4$ teaspoon red pepper flakes

2 cups coconut milk (p. 35)
4 tablespoons (60 gm) butter
  (^{1}/$_2$ stick)
3 onions, sliced into
  paper-thin rings

1. Rinse off the chicken pieces and prick them all over with a fork. Rub the turmeric, pepper and salt, well into the meat. Set aside.

2. Grind or blend the full masala with a spoonful or two of water to make a paste.

3. In a wok or heavy skillet, melt the butter over medium high heat and saute the onions until translucent. Add the masala paste and *bhoona* for 2 minutes.

4. Add the chicken pieces and *bhoona* until golden. Add a few spoonfuls of water if needed to prevent scorching. Add the coconut milk, cover, and simmer until chicken is tender, about 20 minutes.

Korma Badam Malai
CHICKEN IN SAFFRON CREAM

SERVES 4.

1 3-pound (1¹/₂ kg) chicken cut
   into 8 pieces
¹/₄ teaspoon salt
2 cups milk
4 tablespoons (60 gm) butter
   (¹/₂ stick)
3 tablespoons ground almonds
¹/₄ teaspoon ground
   cardamom
3 onions, sliced in paper-thin
   rings

¹/₂ cup raisins
pinch of saffron threads,
   soaked in 2 tablespoons of
   hot water
2 cups heavy cream
¹/₂ cup chicken stock
2 tablespoons chopped
   coriander leaves for garnish

1. Prepare the chicken and place in large pot with water to cover. Bring to a boil, lower heat to medium, cover, simmer for ¹/₂ hour. Drain, reserving ¹/₂ cup of the stock. If there is more save it for another dish. Let chicken cool slightly.

2. Remove skin from chicken and remove meat from the bones. Add the salt and cook the meat in the milk until most of the liquid evaporates, about 20 minutes. Set aside.

3. In a wok or heavy skillet, heat the butter and stir in the almonds, cardamom, and onions. Saute until lightly golden. Stir in the raisins and remove the mixture from the heat.

4. Soak the saffron in the hot water and add the mixture to the heavy cream. Stir into the onion mixture.

5. Preheat oven to 325° F. Butter a large baking dish that has a cover. Spread half the chicken in the dish, cover with half the fried onion mixture. Repeat the layers. Pour chicken stock over the top. Cover the dish and bake for about 20 minutes.

6. Garnish with chopped coriander leaves and serve.

Kesar Murgh
SAFFRON CHICKEN

SERVES 4.

1 roasting chicken, about 3
pounds (1 1/2 kg), cut into 8
pieces
3 tablespoons butter (45 gm)
1 large onion, chopped fine
3 garlic cloves, minced
1 piece of fresh ginger, size of a
walnut, grated

3 green chilies, seeded and
sliced thin
1/2 teaspoon ground
cardamom
1/4 teaspoon saffron threads in
2 tablespoons hot water
1 teaspoon salt

1. Prepare the chicken and set aside.

2. In a wok or heavy skillet heat the butter and saute the onions, garlic, ginger and chilies over medium heat until onions become translucent.

3. Add the saffron water to pan with cardamom, stir well, then add the chicken pieces. Add the salt, cover, and cook over moderate heat for 10 minutes, or until chicken is tender. Uncover, and cook until almost all the liquid evaporates. Serve with rice.

Badami Murgh
SMOTHERED CHICKEN WITH HERBS AND ALMONDS

SERVES 4.

1 3-pound (1¹/₂ kg) chicken,
  skinned and cut into 8
  serving pieces
juice of ¹/₂ lemon
1 teaspoon salt
¹/₂ cup oil
3 tablespoons slivered
  blanched almonds
4 onions, finely chopped
1 tablespoon garlic/ginger
  paste or
  3 garlic cloves, mashed
  1 piece fresh ginger, size of
  walnut, minced
¹/₂ cup hot water
12 blanched almonds, ground

3 tomatoes, chopped

Full Masala:
3 cinnamon sticks, 1 inch long
  (8 cm total)
4 black cardamom pods,
  crushed
4 cloves

Dry Masala:
1 teaspoon ground cumin
2 teaspoons ground coriander
¹/₂ teaspoon turmeric
¹/₂ teaspoon red pepper flakes

chopped coriander leaves for
  garnish (2 tablespoons)

1. Prepare the chicken. Rub well with lemon juice and salt. Cover and let sit at least 2 hours and preferably overnight.

2. In a wok or heavy skillet heat 1 tablespoon oil and saute slivered almonds, stirring constantly, until they are golden, about 3 minutes. Remove and drain on paper towels. Reserve for garnish.

3. Put the remaining oil in the pan and add the onions. Saute onions over medium flame until golden, stirring constantly to prevent scorching.

4. Add garlic/ginger paste and stir-fry for 3 minutes. Add the full masala and cook 2 minutes more.

5. Add chicken pieces, reduce flame to medium and cook until meat turns white—about 5 minutes. Add the dry masala, and stir to blend well. Add the tomatoes, the ground almonds and ¹/₂ cup hot water. Bring to a boil, then reduce heat and simmer, covered, until chicken is tender, about 40 minutes. Check from time to time, adding a few spoonfuls of hot water, if necessary.

6. When chicken is tender, turn off the flame and let the dish cool to room temperature. When ready to serve, heat thoroughly. Serve garnished with the toasted almonds and the coriander.

Murgh Hyderabadi
CHICKEN HYDERABAD STYLE

This is a specialty of the city of Hyderabad, in the central southern state of Andhra Pradesh.

1 3-pound (1 ½ kg) chicken,
   skinned and cut in 8 pieces
1 cup yoghurt
1 ½ teaspoon turmeric
4 tablespoons (60 gm) butter
   (½ stick)
1 onion, sliced thin

Full Masala:
1 tablespoon garlic/ginger
   paste or:
   3 cloves garlic, mashed,

1 piece fresh ginger, size of
   walnut, minced
1 3-inch (8 cm) piece
   cinnamon
2 fresh green chilies, sliced
   thin
6 peppercorns
4 cloves
3 green cardamom pods,
   crushed

3 tomatoes, chopped
salt to taste

1. Prepare the chicken and set aside. Mix yoghurt and turmeric and set aside.

2. Heat the butter and saute the onion until golden. Add the full masala and saute 2 minutes. Add the chicken pieces and saute two minutes longer. Add the tomatoes and salt to taste, then add the yoghurt.

3. Cover and simmer until meat is tender, about 20 minutes.

Murgh Palak
CHICKEN PALAK

1 3-pound (1 ½ kg) chicken,
  skinned and cut into 8
  pieces
4 tablespoons (60 gm) butter
  (½ stick)
2 onions, sliced thin
4 garlic cloves, minced
1 1-inch (3 cm) stick
  cinnamon

Full Masala:
1 piece fresh ginger, size of
  walnut, minced
2 teaspoons coriander seeds

4 tomatoes, chopped
2 cups chopped spinach (or 2
  packages frozen spinach)

1. Prepare chicken and set aside.

2. In a wok or heavy skillet, melt the butter and saute the onions and garlic until translucent. Add the full masala and saute 2 minutes. Add the chicken pieces and saute 2 more minutes, turning to cook chicken on all sides.

3. Put in the tomatoes and the spinach, cover, and simmer until meat is tender, about 20 minutes.

Murgh Foogath
CHICKEN WITH CABBAGE

1 3-pound (1 1/2 kg) chicken,
  skinned and cut into 8
  pieces
1 small cabbage, shredded
4 tablespoons (60 gm) butter
  (1/2 stick)
2 onions, chopped fine
1 tablespoon ginger/garlic
  paste, or

3 garlic cloves, mashed,
1 piece fresh ginger, size of
  walnut, minced
1/2 teaspoon red pepper flakes
1 teaspoon salt
1/2 cup grated fresh coconut
2 tablespoons coriander leaves
  for garnish

1. Boil the chicken in water to cover until tender, about 15 minutes. Remove chicken and reserve stock.

2. Meanwhile, wash and shred the cabbage. Set aside.

3. In a wok or heavy skillet, melt the butter and lightly saute the onions, garlic/ginger paste and pepper flakes for 3 minutes. Stir in the cabbage and the salt. Cook until cabbage has wilted. Stir in the coconut and saute over medium flame for 3 minutes.

4. Add the chicken pieces and the stock and heat through, 5 to 10 minutes.

5. Garnish with the coriander leaves and serve.

NOTE: This dish can also be made substituting green beans, broccoli or other green vegetables for the cabbage.

Moghlai Korma
BRAISED CHICKEN, MOGHUL STYLE

SERVES 4.

1 1½-pound (680 gm) boneless
  chicken breast, skinned
¾ cup oil
6 medium onions, finely
  chopped
1 tablespoon garlic/ginger
  paste or:
  1 piece fresh ginger, size of a
    large walnut, minced
  3 cloves garlic, mashed

Full Masala:
10 cardamom seeds, crushed

15 cloves
2 bay leaves

Dry Masala:
2 teaspoons ground coriander
½ teaspoon red pepper flakes

½ cup yoghurt
½ cup boiling water
1 teaspoon salt
½ cup heavy cream
2 tablespoons chopped fresh
coriander leaves for garnish

1. Slice chicken breasts into ¼-inch (¾ cm) thick medallions, as if for scaloppine. Slice these into 2-inch by 2-inch pieces (6 cm × 6 cm). Set aside.

2. In a wok or heavy skillet heat the oil and add onions and the garlic/ginger paste. Over medium-high heat stir continually until the onions start to turn brown, about 10 minutes. Add the full masala and *bhoona* until bay leaves start to brown, about 5 minutes.

3. Lower heat and add the dry masala and 2 tablespoons of the yoghurt. *Bhoona* until the moisture from the yoghurt evaporates. Add 2 more tablespoons yoghurt and *bhoona*. Continue until all yoghurt is used up, about 5 minutes in all.

4. Add the chicken pieces and stir-fry until meat turns white, about 4 minutes. Add ½ cup boiling water and the salt.

5. Reduce heat to medium low and simmer, covered, until chicken is fork tender, about 20 minutes.

6. Stir in the cream, remove from heat and cool to room temperature. When ready to serve, reheat thoroughly, and serve at once. Garnish with chopped coriander leaves.

Murgh Malai
CHICKEN IN COCONUT SAUCE

SERVES 4.

2 whole chicken breasts,
    skinned, about 2 pounds (1
    kg)
1/2 cup oil
1 large onion, chopped fine
2 tablespoons garlic/ginger
    paste or
    6 cloves garlic, mashed
    1 piece fresh ginger, size of
      Brazil nut, minced
2 tablespoons blanched
    almonds, ground

Full Masala:
3 1-inch (3 cm) cinnamon
    sticks

12 cloves
6 green cardamom pods,
    crushed

1 1/2 cups coconut milk

Dry Masala:
1 teaspoon salt
1/2 teaspoon red pepper flakes
1/4 teaspoon turmeric

1/3 cup heavy cream
2 tablespoons chopped
    coriander leaves for garnish

1. Prepare chicken. Do not remove bones. Set aside.

2. In a wok or heavy skillet, heat the oil and add the onions and the garlic/ginger mixture. Over medium-high flame, saute until onions become translucent—about 5 minutes. Add the full masala and saute until spices begin to dance, about 3 minutes. Add the ground almonds and stir for 2 minutes.

3. Reduce heat to medium and add chicken pieces in a single layer. Cook the chicken on both sides until it loses its pinkness, about 2 minutes to a side. The chicken should not be allowed to brown.

4. Add the coconut milk and the dry masala and bring to a boil. Reduce heat and simmer, covered, until chicken is tender, about 25 minutes. Check often and add a few spoons of water if the dish begins to dry out. When the chicken is done, gently stir in the cream and turn off the heat.

5. Let the dish rest for about 1 hour. When ready to serve, heat thoroughly. Garnish with the coriander leaves.

Aru Murgh
CHICKEN WITH APRICOTS

SERVES 4.

1 3-pound (1¹/₂ kg) chicken,
   skinned and cut into 8
   pieces

Masala Paste:
2 green chilies
2 garlic cloves
1 teaspoon cumin seeds

4 tablespoons (60 gm) butter
   (¹/₂ stick)

2 onions, sliced thin
4 tomatoes, chopped
4 apricots, pits removed,
   chopped
salt to taste
¹/₂ cup water
2 tablespoons chopped
   coriander leaves for garnish

1. Prepare the chicken and set aside.

2. Grind the masala in a mortar or add a little water and make it into a paste in a blender. Set aside.

3. In a wok or heavy skillet, melt butter and saute the onions until golden. Add the chicken pieces and *bhoona* over medium heat until chicken is brown, about 10 minutes. Add the masala paste, the tomatoes, apricots and salt, plus ¹/₂ cup of water. Simmer until meat is tender, 15–20 minutes.

4. Garnish with coriander leaves and serve.

Batakh Buffado
SPICY DUCK WITH CABBAGE AND POTATOES

SERVES 4.

1 4-pound (2 kg) duck,
  skinned and cut into 8
  serving pieces
2 tablespoons oil
1 large onion, sliced into
  paper-thin rings

Full Masala
1 3-inch stick cinnamon (8
  cm)
4 cardamom pods, crushed
4 cloves

1 piece fresh ginger, size of
  almond, minced
1 garlic clove, mashed

Dry Masala:
2 teaspoons ground coriander
1 teaspoon ground turmeric
generous grinding black
  pepper

3 fresh red chilies or 2
  teaspoons red pepper flakes
1 teaspoon salt
2 tablespoons white vinegar
2 cups hot water
4 small potatoes, peeled
half a cabbage head, cut into
  wedges
1 cup fresh green peas (or 1
  package frozen)

1. Skin and prepare duck and set aside.

2. In a wok or heavy skillet heat the oil and saute the onion rings and full masala until onions turn golden.

3. Add ginger and garlic and the dry masala and stir to blend. Add duck pieces, and turn until duck becomes slightly brown. Add the chilies, salt, vinegar and 2 cups of hot water. Cover and simmer 45 minutes or until duck is tender. Skim off fat.

4. Add potatoes and cook 10 minutes, uncovered. Add cabbage and cook another 10 minutes. Add peas, adjust seasoning and serve.

Vathoo Kari
SOUTH INDIA DUCK CURRY

To enjoy this spicy curry at its best, serve it simply with plain steamed rice and some chutneys or pappadums on the side.

SERVES 4.

1 4-pound (2 kg) duck,
    skinned and cut into 8
    serving pieces
2 tablespoons (30 gm) butter
    (1/4 stick)
2 onions, chopped fine
1 tablespoon garlic/ginger
    paste or
    3 garlic cloves, mashed
    1 piece fresh ginger, size of
    walnut, mashed

Dry Masala:
1 1/2 teaspoons turmeric
1/2 teaspoon ground coriander
1 teaspoon ground cumin
1 teaspoon red pepper flakes
1/2 teaspoon ground fenugreek

2 1/2 cups thin coconut milk
3 green chilies, seeded and
    sliced thin lengthwise
1 teaspoon salt
juice of 1/2 lemon

1. Prepare the duck and set aside.

2. In a wok or heavy skillet, heat the butter and add the onions and the garlic/ginger paste. Stir-fry until onions are golden.

3. Mix the dry masala with a little of the coconut milk to form a paste. Add the paste to the duck and *bhoona* for 8 minutes. Add the coconut milk, salt, and chilies. Bring curry to a boil, then cover, and reduce heat to low.

4. Simmer until duck is tender, about 45 minutes. Stir in lemon juice and salt.

Khata Batakh Vindaloo
HOT AND SOUR DUCK VINDALOO

1 4-pound (2 kg) duck,
   skinned and cut into 8
   serving pieces
8 dried red chilies
$^1/_2$ cup vinegar
2 tablespoons garlic/ginger
   paste or
   6 garlic cloves, mashed
   1 piece of fresh ginger, size
     of Brazil nut, mashed

Dry Masala:
1 tablespoon ground coriander
1 tablespoon ground cumin
1 teaspoon turmeric
generous grinding black
   pepper

2 tablespoons (30 gm) butter
   ($^1/_4$ stick)
1 teaspoon salt
$^1/_2$ cup hot water
1 or 2 teaspoons sugar

1. Prepare duck, removing most of the fat. Remove seeds and stems from dried red chilies and soak chilies in vinegar for 10 minutes.

2. Place the chilies and the garlic/ginger paste in a blender and puree with the vinegar. Scrape mixture into a large bowl and add the dry masala. Add the duck pieces and coat well. Cover and marinate for 2 hours at room temperature, or overnight in refrigerator.

3. In a wok or heavy skillet, heat the butter and saute the duck pieces until light golden; add salt and $^1/_2$ cup hot water, along with any leftover marinade. Cover and simmer until duck is tender, about $1^1/_2$ hours. Turn duck occasionally; when it is tender add 1 or 2 teaspoons of sugar. Stir well and serve.

Batakh Vindaloo
DUCK VINDALOO

SERVES 8.

1 4-pound (2 kg) duck,
   skinned and cut into 8
   serving pieces

First Full Masala:
2 cinnamon sticks, 1 inch long
   (3 cm)
2 bay leaves
2 cardamom seeds, crushed
2 cloves

4 cups water
1 large potato, parboiled,
   peeled and cut into 1-inch (3
   cm) cubes
2 large onions, chopped

Second Full Masala:
3 garlic cloves, mashed
1 piece fresh ginger, size of a
   walnut, minced
1 1/4 teaspoon cumin seeds
1 1/4 teaspoon coriander seeds
1 teaspoon poppy seeds
3 red chilies, mashed
3/4 teaspoon turmeric
3/4 teaspoon garam masala
1 1/4 teaspoons salt

1 cup white vinegar
3 tablespoons butter (45 gm)
1/2 teaspoon or more sugar
   (optional)
1 tablespoon chopped fresh
   green chilies, for garnish

1. Prepare the duck, removing most of the fat. Place the duck, the first full masala, and 4 cups of water, into a wok or large pot and bring to a boil. Turn heat to low and simmer until meat is tender, about 1 1/2 hours. Drain, reserving the liquid.

2. Meanwhile, prepare the potato and set aside.

3. Put the onions, the second full masala and 1/2 cup of the vinegar into a food processor or blender and puree.

4. In a wok or heavy skillet melt the butter and saute the duck pieces until golden, about 15 minutes. Remove from pan and drain on paper towels.

5. Add the pureed spice mixture and the cubed potato to the pan and stir gently, for 2 minutes. Return the duck to the pan. Rinse the blender bowl with the rest of the vinegar and add to the duck. Add the sugar (if used).

6. Simmer for 20 minutes and taste for tartness. You may want to add 1/2 teaspoon or more of sugar or a dash more vinegar, according to taste, at this point. Garnish with the chopped chilies and serve.

Chapter 7

MEAT
SPECIALTIES

A great many Indians do not eat meat at all. The Hindus consider most animals to be sacred, especially the cow, and they abstain from eating meat on religious grounds. Others are largely vegetarian, either for economic reasons or because vegetarianism is a natural outgrowth of their sense of reverence for life. This is especially true for many holy men.

Matters are even more complicated because Moslems and Jews are not permitted to eat pork, while Christians enjoy meats of all kinds.

Certainly lamb or mutton plays a great role in the Indian cuisine of the North, again doubtless part of the Punjabi inheritance from the ancient Persians. While lamb is the preferred meat for most of the following recipes, tender American beef (especially chopped beef) can often be satisfactorily substituted.

Rogan Gosht
LAMB CURRY WITH MILD SPICES & YOGHURT

This is one of the dishes ordered most often from a Bombay Palace menu.

2 pounds (1 kg) baby lamb, all
  fat removed, boned, and cut
  into 2-inch (5 cm) cubes
2 potatoes, peeled and
  quartered
1/2 cup oil
2 medium onions, cut into
  paper-thin rings, then
  halved
2 ripe tomatoes, crushed
1 tablespoon garlic/ginger
  paste, or
  3 garlic cloves, mashed
  1 piece fresh ginger, size of
    walnut, minced

Full Masala:
1 3-inch (8 cm) cinnamon
  stick, broken into pieces
4 cloves
2 black cardamom pods,
  crushed
2 green cardamom pods,
  crushed

1 teaspoon dried chili
  pepper flakes (equal to 2
  dried pods)
1/2 teaspoon cumin seeds
1/2 teaspoon coriander seeds
2 bay leaves, crumbled
salt and fresh-ground pepper
  to taste

Dry Masala:
1 teaspoon turmeric
1/2 teaspoon ground
  coriander
1/2 teaspoon ground cumin
1/2 teaspoon paprika
1/4 teaspoon red chili
  powder

1/2 cup yoghurt
1 cup water

1 rounded teaspoon garam
  masala
2 tablespoons coriander
  Garnish:

1. Prepare lamb and set aside.

2. Drop potatoes in boiling water and boil 5 minutes. Drain and set aside.

3. In a wok or heavy skillet heat the oil and saute the onions, stirring constantly until they start to turn dark brown. Do not scorch.

4. Add the tomatoes, garlic/ginger paste, and the full masala. *Bhoona* (see p. 13), stirring frequently until mixture becomes a paste.

5. Add the lamb cubes and stir gently for 2 minutes, then add the dry masala. Add 1/2 cup water and *bhoona* for 20 minutes, being careful not to let the mixture scorch. If it becomes too dry, add a spoonful of water from time to time.

6. Stir in the yoghurt and simmer for 5 minutes. Add about 1/2 cup water (depending on how thick you prefer your gravy), cover, and simmer until meat becomes tender, about 20 minutes.

7. Sprinkle garam masala over the top, garnish with coriander leaves.

Gosht Do Piaza
LAMB WITH ONIONS COOKED IN TWO STYLES

As with Chicken Do Piaza (p. 68), *Do Piaza* translates as "with two onions," even though three onions are actually called for. The real meaning is that onions cooked in two different styles are used in the same dish. Beef may also be used for this recipe instead of lamb.

SERVES 4.

2 pounds (1 kg) lamb,
   trimmed of all fat and cut
   into 1¹/₂-inch (4 cm) cubes;
   or substitute
   2 pounds (1 kg) sirloin,
   trimmed and cubed
3 large onions, sliced in
   paper-thin rings
¹/₂ cup oil

Full Masala:
1 tablespoon cumin seeds
12 whole cloves
8 green cardmom pods,
   crushed
6 black cardmom pods,
   crushed, or
   18 green pods
1 tablespoon garlic/ginger
   paste or
   3 garlic cloves, mashed

1 piece fresh ginger, size of
   walnut, minced
2 tomatoes, chopped

Dry Masala:
2 teaspoons ground cumin
1 teaspoon paprika
1 teaspoon ground coriander
1 teaspoon turmeric
1 teaspoon garam masala
¹/₂ teaspoon red chili powder

3 cups water
1 teaspoon salt and generous
   grinding fresh pepper
4 tablespoons yoghurt
4 tablespoons heavy cream
1 tablespoon cashews, mixed
   with a bit of water and
   mashed to a paste
2 tablespoons chopped
   coriander leaves for garnish

1. Prepare meat and set aside. Prepare onions (see p. 68).

2. In a wok or heavy skillet, heat 1 tablespoon of the oil and saute one half of the onions until they turn dark brown and crisp. Do not scorch. Set aside to drain on paper towels.

3. Add the rest of the oil and when it is hot add the full masala and the rest of the onions. *Bhoona* until onions start to turn brown, then add the garlic/ginger paste and the tomatoes. *Bhoona* for 5 minutes (see p. 13).

4. Add the meat, stirring to coat with spices. Add dry masala and *bhoona* 5 minutes. Add ¼ cup of water while stirring if necessary to prevent sticking. Now add 3 cups water, bring to boil, cover, and simmer until liquid is reduced by half, about 20 minutes.

5. Add salt and pepper, yoghurt, cream, and cashew paste. Stir the mixture over heat for 3 minutes.

6. Garnish with coriander leaves and serve.

Badsahi Badam Korma
LAMB CURRY WITH ALMONDS

SERVES 6.

2 pounds (1 kg) leg of lamb, trimmed of all fat, cut into 2-inch (5 cm) cubes
10 garlic cloves, crushed
6 tablespoons (90 gm) butter
4 onions, thinly sliced
½ cup slivered almonds
1 piece fresh ginger, size of Brazil nut, minced
1 bay leaf

Dry Masala:
1 teaspoon ground cumin
½ teaspoon turmeric
½ teaspoon red chili powder
½ teaspoon ground cardamom

½ teaspoon salt
1 cup yoghurt

1. Prepare the lamb. Set aside.

2. Soak garlic cloves in ½ cup boiling water for ½ hour. Drain, reserving liquid; discard garlic.

3. In a wok or heavy skillet heat the butter and saute half the onions until golden. Remove with slotted spoon and set aside.

4. Saute the almonds in the butter until light brown. Remove with slotted spoon and set aside.

5. Put the remaining onions, ginger and bay leaf into the pan. Saute for 2 minutes, adding more butter if necessary.

6. Add the lamb cubes and the dry masala and the salt. Cook over low heat, sprinkling with garlic water occasionally, until meat is brown, about 6 minutes. Do not allow meat to burn. Cover and simmer for 1 hour, or until meat is tender. Add the fried onions and almonds, and mix in the yoghurt. Simmer for 5 minutes and serve.

91

Mahns Kashmiri
LAMB, KASHMIRI STYLE

SERVES 4.

2 pounds (1 kg) leg of lamb,
  trimmed of fat, flattened
  and cut into bite-sized
  pieces

Full Masala:
2 tablespoons garlic/ginger
  paste or
  6 garlic cloves, mashed
  1 piece fresh ginger, size of
    Brazil nut, minced
1 2-inch (5 cm) cinnamon
  stick, broken
1 tablespoon fennel seeds
6 black peppercorns, crushed

2 dried red chilis, crushed
4 cloves
4 cardamom pods, crushed

2 cups yoghurt
1/4 teaspoon saffron threads,
  soaked in 2 tablespoons
  warm water
1 tablespoon lemon juice
4 tablespoons (60 gm) butter
  (1/2 stick)
1/2 cup almonds, blanched and
  chopped
1/2 cup cashews, chopped

1. Prepare lamb. Flatten lamb with a mallet. Slice into bite-sized pieces. Set aside.

2. In a blender or spice mill grind the full masala and stir into the yoghurt. Marinate the meat in the yoghurt mixture for at least 1 hour.

3. Meanwhile, soak the saffron and add the lemon juice.

4. Put the meat and the marinade into a wok or heavy skillet and simmer, covered, until liquid is evaporated. Add the saffron liquid and butter. Saute over medium heat until the meat is nicely browned, about 5 minutes.

5. In a separate pan saute the nuts in a little butter until they are golden.

6. When the meat is tender, about 15 minutes, garnish with the golden nuts and serve.

Anda Mahns
LAMB WITH EGG SAUCE

SERVES 4.

2 pounds (1 kg) leg of lamb,
  boned, trimmed of fat and
  cut into 2-inch (5 cm) cubes
4 potatoes, peeled and
  quartered
4 tablespoons (60 gms) butter
  (1/2 stick)
4 onions, chopped fine
8 cloves garlic, chopped fine

Full Masala:
1 3-inch (8 cm) piece of
  cinnamon, broken
8 cloves, whole
2 red chilies, seeded and
  crushed
2 teaspoons fennel seeds
2 teaspoons turmeric

1/4 cup water
2 eggs
1 cup coconut milk (p. 35)
Juice of 1 lemon

1. Prepare meat and set aside. Parboil potatoes by putting them in cold water to cover, bringing them to a boil, then draining. Set aside.

2. In a wok or heavy skillet melt the butter and saute onion and garlic until golden. Add the full masala and *bhoona* for 2 minutes. Add the meat and brown lightly. Add 1/4 cup water and simmer gently until meat is tender, about 15 minutes. Add a bit more water if needed.

3. While the lamb cooks, beat the eggs, gradually adding the coconut milk. Add lemon juice and mix well. Pour the sauce over the meat. Add the potatoes, cover, and simmer until meat and vegetables are tender, 10-15 minutes. Keep the gravy thick, but add a bit of water if necessary to prevent scorching.

Mahns Phali
LAMB AND GREEN BEANS

SERVES 4-6.

2 pounds (1 kg) lamb, boned,
   trimmed of fat, and cut into
   1-inch (3 cm) cubes
2 ounces (60 gm) butter (1/2
   stick)
4 onions, sliced thin
2 pounds green beans, sliced
   thin lengthwise (1 kg)
generous grinding of black
   pepper and salt to taste

Dry Masala:
1/4 teaspoon each of ground:
   coriander
   cumin
   paprika
   red chili powder
   turmeric

1. Prepare lamb and set aside.

2. In a wok or heavy skillet melt the butter and saute the lamb, turning to brown all sides. Add the onions and saute until translucent. Add the beans and stir-fry for 3 minutes.

3. Sprinkle with the dry masala and 1/4 cup water. Cover, and simmer until meat is tender, about 15 minutes.

Raan Pasanda
LAMB CUTLETS IN FRAGRANT CREAM SAUCE

2 pounds (1 kg) leg of lamb,
   cut into 3/4-inch (2 cm)
   cutlets

Marinade:
1/2 teaspoon salt
generous grinding of
   fresh-milled pepper
4 ounces (120 gm) yoghurt

1/4 teaspoon ground
   cardamom

Cream Sauce:
1 cup milk
4 ounces (120 gm) cashews
2 ounces (60 gm) yoghurt
1/4 teaspoon salt
grinding of fresh-milled pepper
2 ounces (60 gm) heavy cream

1. Tenderize the lamb cutlets by scoring them lightly in a crisscross pattern with a very sharp knife. Rub the marinade into the lamb and lay the lamb in a single layer in a casserole or baking pan. Let the meat sit in the marinade for 1/2 hour to 1 hour.

2. Preheat oven to 400°F. Bake the lamb for 15 minutes, then turn the oven off and let the meat sit for 10 minutes.

3. Make the sauce by putting the milk and the cashews in a blender. Puree to make a thin paste. In a small saucepan, put the remaining sauce ingredients. Stir in the milk-nut paste and mix well. Bring to a boil, then simmer for 2 minutes. Add this mixture to the meat and its pan juices. Bring just to a boil and serve at once.

Raan
ROAST LEG OF LAMB, KASHMIRI STYLE

NOTE: The meat should be allowed to marinate overnight, or even longer, to gain its full flavor.

SERVES 8.

1 5-pound (2 ¹/₄ kg) leg of
  lamb

Marinade:
1 tablespoon garlic/ginger
  paste or
  3 garlic cloves, mashed
  1 piece fresh ginger, size of
    walnut, minced
1 teaspoon salt

Dry Masala:
1 teaspoon ground cumin

1 teaspoon turmeric
¹/₂ teaspoon ground cinnamon
¹/₂ teaspoon ground
  cardamom
¹/₂ teaspoon red chili powder
¹/₄ teaspoon ground cloves

juice of ¹/₂ lemon
¹/₂ teaspoon saffron threads
³/₄ cup yoghurt
2 tablespoons each blanched
  almonds and pistachios
1 tablespoon honey

1. Trim all fat from lamb, and, using a sharp knife, make slits all over the leg.

2. Combine the garlic/ginger paste and the salt with the dry masala and lemon juice to make a paste. If paste seems too thick, add more lemon juice. Spread the paste over the meat, forcing it into each slit.

3. Soak the saffron threads in hot water for 5 minutes.

4. In a blender or food processor put the yoghurt, the blanched nuts and the saffron threads with their water, and puree. Coat the lamb with the puree. Drizzle honey over the meat.

5. It is best to marinate the meat for two days in the refrigerator, or at least overnight. Cover loosely.

6. Preheat oven to 450° F and roast lamb in a covered baking dish (use foil wrap if necessary) for ¹/₂ hour. Reduce heat to 325° F and cook at 25 minutes to the pound, about 1¹/₂ hours, until meat is tender.

Lamb roasted in this way is traditionally served at room temperature, but may be served hot if preferred.

Kamargah
LAMB CHOPS IN SPICY BATTER

Marinating lamb in milk and spices is a typical Kashmiri cooking technique.

SERVES 4.

8 lamb chops, trimmed except
   for a thin rim of fat

Marinade:
1 1/2 cups milk

Full Masala:
1 3-inch (8 cm) piece of
   cinnamon
12 black peppercorns
8 cardamom pods, crushed
8 whole cloves

Batter:
1/3 cup besan (chick-pea flour)
1/3 cup water

Dry Masala:
1 teaspoon ground coriander
1/2 teaspoon salt
1/4 teaspoon each of ground
   cardamom, cinnamon,
   cloves, nutmeg, turmeric
1/4 teaspoon red chili flakes
1 tablespoon butter for frying

1. Prepare the lamb chops. Mix the milk and full masala to prepare marinade.

2. Place the chops and the marinade in a wok or heavy skillet. Bring to a boil, reduce heat, cover, and simmer until meat is tender and liquid evaporates, about 20 minutes. Set aside.

3. Prepare batter, and beat to blend well. Let stand for 1/2 hour. Dip the chops in the batter, coating them thinly.

4. Heat the butter, which should just cover the bottom of a heavy skillet. Fry the chops, 4 at a time, until golden brown on both sides. Drain on paper towels.

5. Serve with one or more vegetable side dishes.

Raan Korma
LAMB CHOPS WITH SPICES & YOGHURT

SERVES 4.

8 lamb chops, trimmed except
   for a thin rim of fat.
4 tablespoons (60 gm) yoghurt
1 cup water
3 tablespoons oil

Full Masala:
2 3-inch (8 cm) cinnamon
   sticks, broken
12 black peppercorns
8 whole cloves
8 cardamom pods, crushed
2 bay leaves
2 dried red chilies, crushed

1 tablespoon garlic/ginger
   paste, or
   3 garlic cloves, mashed
   1 piece fresh ginger, size of
     walnut, minced
1 teaspoon salt

2 tablespoons chopped
   coriander leaves (or
   substitute mint) for garnish

1. Prepare lamb chops and set aside.

2. In a ceramic or glass bowl, mix the yoghurt with 1 cup water and set aside.

3. In a wok or heavy skillet heat the oil. Put in 4 of the chops and brown on both sides. Remove with a slotted spoon and set aside in a bowl. Repeat with second set of chops.

4. Put the full masala into the pot and *bhoona* 20 seconds. Add the gar-lic/ginger paste and *bhoona* 1 minute.

5. Return the lamb chops to the pot, together with any liquid accumulated in the bowl. Stir up the yoghurt mixture and pour over chops. Add the salt and bring mixture to a boil. Cover and simmer 40 minutes, stirring gently occasionally.

6. Garnish with the coriander and serve.

Sookah Keema
MINCED LAMB OR BEEF

This traditional dish has many useful variations. This particular recipe makes a fine main entree. Keema can also be stirred into a vegetable dish of your liking. It makes a superb stuffing for breads and samosas. It can be used to stuff vegetables, such as eggplant, green peppers or zucchini. Finally, when gently stirred into cooked rice it becomes a keema pulao. This same recipe can also be adapted to create interesting dishes from other cuisines, particularly those of the Middle East.

SERVES 4.

1 pound (1/2 kg) ground lamb
   or beef
2 tablespoons oil
2 onions, chopped fine
2 fresh green chilies, seeded
   and chopped fine
1 tablespoon garlic/ginger
   paste, or:
   3 cloves garlic, mashed
   1 piece fresh ginger, size of
     walnut, chopped fine

Full Masala:
1 3-inch (8 cm) cinnamon
   stick

2 black cardamom pods,
   crushed
2 green cardamom pods,
   crushed
4 cloves
1/2 teaspoon cumin seds
1/2 teaspoon coriander seeds
2 dried chili pods, crushed
1 bay leaf, crumbled

1/2 teaspoon salt
1/4 teaspoon turmeric
2 teaspoons lemon juice

2 tablespoons chopped
   coriander leaves for garnish

1. Avoid using hamburger. For better texture, have the meat coarse-ground by the butcher or do it yourself in a food processor or meat grinder. Set aside.

2. In a wok or heavy skillet heat the oil and saute the onions over medium-high heat until they begin to caramelize, about 8 minutes. Stir constantly so they will brown evenly without scorching.

3. Add the green chilies and ginger/garlic paste and cook 2 minutes. Add the ground meat and stir until it loses its pink color.

4. Sprinkle on the full masala, and *bhoona* 3 minutes, stirring constantly. Sprinkle in the salt and the turmeric and add ¼ cup water. (For *bhoona* technique, see p. 13.)

5. Reduce heat, cover, and simmer 20-25 minutes. Stir often to prevent scorching. All the moisture should be absorbed. If it is not, uncover the pan, raise the heat and stir until the moisture evaporates. Turn off the heat, add lemon juice and mix well.

6. Garnish with coriander leaves and serve.

NOTE: If you prefer a moist keema, cook only about 15 minutes. For use as a stuffing, keema should not be moist.

Keema Matar
GROUND MEAT WITH FRIED ONIONS AND PEAS

This is one of the many variations on the keema theme. It is worth making this dish for comparison, to see how a classic Indian dish always allows room for a classic variation. Because of the tomato sauce, this version is more moist than the similar keema recipe on page 99.

SERVES 4-6.

Follow the recipe for Sookah Keema (minced lamb/beef) above, making the following changes:

1. Before preparing the meat dish, slice 1 medium onion into very thin slices. Separate into rings and in a wok or skillet heat a little oil and fry the rings for about 5 minutes, until they are dark brown, but not burnt. Set aside to drain on paper towels.

2. In step 4 of the Sookah Keema recipe, instead of adding water, substitute ⅓ cup tomato sauce. At this point also add a generous grinding of fresh nutmeg—at least ½ teaspoonful.

3. Just before the dish is completely cooked, add 1 cup of fresh peas (or 1 package frozen), re-cover and simmer for 3 minutes until peas are just tender.

4. Sprinkle the dark-fried onion rings over the top of the dish and serve.

Keema Masala
SPICY MINCED LAMB OR BEEF

NOTE: This dish can also be prepared using chicken. See suggestion on page 66.

SERVES 4-6.

2 pounds (1 kg) boneless lamb
  or beef, trimmed of all fat,
  and put through fine blade
  of meat grinder or shredded
  in a food processor
2 ounces (60 gm) cashew nuts,
  ground to a paste
1/4 cup oil
4 hardboiled eggs (optional)

Full Masala
1 3-inch (8 cm) cinnamon
  stick, broken
4 whole cloves
2 green cardamom pods,
  crushed
1/2 teaspoon cumin seed
3 medium onions, chopped
  fine

Dry Masala:
1 teaspoon garam masala
  (p.16)
1/2 teaspoon ground coriander
1/2 teaspoon ground cumin

1/2 teaspoon turmeric
1/2 teaspoon paprika
1/4 teaspoon red chili powder
1/4 teaspoon salt
generous grinding black
  pepper

3 tomatoes, chopped
3 medium potatoes, peeled
  and cut into quarters
1 tablespoon garlic/ginger
  paste, or
  3 garlic cloves, mashed
  1 piece fresh ginger, size of
    walnut, minced
1 cup yoghurt
1 cup water
4 tablespoons heavy cream
1 1/2 cups fresh peas (or 1
  package frozen)

4 hardboiled eggs for garnish
  (optional)
2 tablespoons coriander leaves
  for garnish

1. Prepare meat and set aside. Grind cashews in mortar with pestle, or, in blender with a bit of water. Set aside.

2. In a wok or heavy skillet heat the oil and add the full masala, stirring constantly for 1/2 minute. Add the onions and the dry masala, stir-fry 1 minute. Add the ground meat and *bhoona* until meat looses its redness, about 2 minutes. (For *bhoona*-ing see p. 13.)

3. Add the tomatoes, potatoes, and the garlic/ginger paste and *bhoona* 5 minutes to dry the mixture. Stir con-

stantly to avoid scorching. Add 1/2 cup water and simmer 5 minutes, until mixture again becomes dry.

4. Add yoghurt and *bhoona* 2 minutes. Add the cashew paste and *bhoona* 1/2 minute. Add 1/2 cup water and simmer 5 minutes. Add the cream and mix well. Add the peas and mix well. (If using the eggs, slice them in half, lengthwise, and add them when you add the peas.) Simmer for 5 minutes until peas are barely cooked and the mixture is dry. (NOTE: Traditionally the keema masala should be dry. If you like gravy, add a little water, about 1/4 cup, when you add the peas and eggs.)

5. Garnish with coriander leaves, and serve.

Gosht Curry
BEEF CURRY

SERVES 4-6.

2 pounds (1 kg) beef, trimmed
   of all fat, cut into 2-inch (5
   cm) cubes
4 tablespoons (50 gm) butter
   (1/2 stick)
4 onions, chopped
2 cloves garlic, minced
1 cup yoghurt

Dry Masala:
2 teaspoons ground coriander

1 teaspoon ground ginger
1/2 teaspoon ground
   cardamom
1/2 teaspoon ground cinnamon
1/2 teaspoon ground cloves
1/2 teaspoon red chili powder
   (or more, as desired)
1 bay leaf

salt and freshly ground pepper
   to taste

1. Prepare meat and set aside.

2. In a wok or heavy skillet, melt the butter and the onions and saute until golden. Add the garlic and saute 1 minute. Remove the onion mixture and set aside.

3. Add the meat to the pan and brown on all sides. Reduce the flame and add all remaining ingredients but 1 tablespoon of the onions, reserving that for garnish. Cover and simmer for 20 minutes, or until meat is tender.

4. Remove the curry to a warmed serving dish, sprinkle the spoonful of onions on top, and serve.

Gosht Vindaloo
BEEF VINDALOO

Duck or pork are usually used in this Portuguese dish from Goa, but here is a spicy variation for beef lovers.

SERVES 6-8.

2 pounds (1 kg) stewing beef, trimmed of all fat and cut into 2-inch (5 cm) cubes
1 onion, coarsely chopped
3 garlic cloves

Full Masala:
2 tablespoons coriander seeds
1 tablespoon turmeric
2 teaspoons red pepper flakes

1 teaspoon powdered ginger
1/2 teaspoon cumin seeds
1/2 teaspoon fenugreek seeds
1/2 teaspoon mustard seeds
1/4 cup vinegar to make a paste

4 tablespoons (60 gm) butter (1/2 stick)

1. Prepare beef and set aside.

2. Put the onion, garlic and the full masala in a blender. Blend, adding enough vinegar to make a thick paste.

3. Put the meat in a large bowl and coat well with the masala paste. Marinate at least 4 hours and preferably overnight.

4. In a wok or heavy skillet melt the butter and brown the beef over high heat. Then lower flame. Simmer until tender, about 1 1/2 hours, stirring occasionally.

NOTE: In Goa you would probably use an additional teaspoon of the pepper flakes.

Moghlai Frezie
BEEF COCONUT CURRY

SERVES 4-6.

2 pounds (1 kg) stewing beef,
   trimmed of all fat, cut into
   2-inch cubes (5 cm)
1 cup coconut milk (p. 35)
4 tablespoons (60 gm) butter
   (¹/₂ stick)
2 onions, sliced thin
2 tablespoons garlic/ginger
   paste, or
   6 garlic cloves, mashed
   1 piece fresh ginger, size of
   Brazil nut, mashed

Full Masala:
1 3-inch (8 cm) piece
   cinnamon, broken into
   pieces

2 bay leaves, crushed
2 red chilies, crushed
2 cardamom pods, crushed

Dry Masala:
 1¹/₂ teaspoons ground
   coriander
1¹/₂ teaspoons ground cumin
¹/₄ teaspoon red chili powder
¹/₄ teaspoon turmeric
¹/₄ teaspoon paprika

1 teaspoon salt
1¹/₂ tablespoons tomato paste
1 cup yoghurt
2 tablespoons chopped
   coriander leaves for garnish

1. Prepare meat and set aside.

2. In a saucepan bring coconut milk to a boil, add the beef cubes, cover, and cook over medium heat until meat is almost tender, about 30 minutes. Drain, and discard coconut milk.

3. In a wok or heavy skillet, heat the butter and saute onions until translucent. Remove onions with slotted spoon and set aside.

4. Add the garlic/ginger paste, the full masala and the dry masala, and *bhoona* 1 minute. Add the beef, salt and tomato paste and saute gently until mixture is a golden brown color, about 10 minutes. Stir in the yoghurt, add the fried onions and simmer, uncovered, 20 minutes. Garnish with coriander leaves and serve.

Jeera Mira
CUMIN BEEF

SERVES 4.

2 pounds (1 kg) top round
   beef, trimmed of all fat and
   cut into 2-inch (5 cm) cubes.
4 tablespoons (60 gm) butter
   ($^1/_2$ stick)
2 onions, sliced thin
1 tablespoon garlic/ginger
   paste, or
   3 garlic cloves, mashed
   1 piece fresh ginger, size of
   walnut, minced

Dry Masala:
1 tablespoon ground cumin
1 teaspoon turmeric
generous grinding of black
   pepper

salt to taste
4 tablespoons white vinegar.
$^1/_4$ cup water

1. Prepare the meat and set aside.

2. In a wok or heavy skillet, melt the butter and saute the onion until translucent. Add the meat and all the ingredients except the salt and vinegar.

3. Brown meat over medium heat.

4. Add the salt, vinegar and about $^1/_4$ cup water, and saute gently until meat is tender, about 20 minutes.

Keema Methi Baji
MINCED MEAT WITH FENUGREEK

SERVES 4.

1 pound (¹/₂ kg) beefsteak
2 pounds (1 kg) fenugreek
  leaves, or substitute spinach
  or collards
4 tablespoons (60 gm) butter
  (¹/₂ stick)
2 onions, chopped fine
4 fresh green chilies, seeded
  and sliced

1 tablespoon garlic/ginger
  paste, or
  3 garlic cloves, mashed
  1 piece fresh ginger, size of
    walnut, minced
salt to taste

1. Trim the beef of all fat and, using a sharp knife, slice meat rapidly until it is in fine shreds. Set aside.

2. Soak the fenugreek in water to cover and set aside.

3. In a wok or heavy skillet, melt the butter and saute the onion until trans-lucent. Add the meat, the green chilies and the garlic/ginger paste. Saute until the meat loses its redness.

4. Drain the fenugreek, chop coarse-ly, and add to wok. Sprinkle with salt. Cover and simmer a few minutes until vegetable is tender.

Pork Vindaloo

While pork is not eaten throughout India, it is one of the chief meats in Goa, the trader's port first entered from the West by the Portuguese, centuries ago. Goa has developed a mini-cuisine of its own, and vindaloo is one of its chief creations, a dish that has become popular in Indian restaurants everywhere. True vindaloos are characterized by two things: the technique of marinating a meat in vinegar, and the addition of extremely fiery spices. While this traditional dish features pork, duck is also widely used for vindaloo; or you may substitute a meat of your choice. In Goa, the following recipe would be more hotly spiced. In most Indian restaurants, vindaloo signifies the spiciest type of dish on the menu.

NOTE: The meat in the recipe must be marinated for 12 hours.

SERVES 4.

2 pounds (1 kg) pork, trimmed of all fat and cut into 2-inch (5 cm) cubes

Full Masala:
2 tablespoons coriander seeds
1 tablespoon cumin seeds
1 1-inch (3 cm) cinnamon stick
6 cloves
6 black peppercorns
2 green cardamom pods, crushed

Dry Masala:
2 tablespoons turmeric

1 tablespoon red chili flakes
1 teaspoon paprika
1 teaspoon ground coriander
1 teaspoon salt
3 tablespoons garlic/ginger paste or
   9 garlic cloves, mashed
   fresh ginger, size of Brazil nut, minced
white vinegar

2 bay leaves, crushed
5 cloves garlic
2 tablespoons (30 gm) butter (¹/₄ stick)
2 teaspoons mustard seeds

1. Prepare meat and set aside.

2. Lightly roast the full masala in a dry skillet, until seeds begin to change color. Remove from pan, grind, and combine with dry masala and garlic/ginger mixture to make a thick paste. Slash meat with a sharp knife and rub the spice paste well into the crevices. Sprinkle crushed bay leaves over the meat and cover with vinegar. Marinate overnight.

3. When ready to cook, crush the garlic cloves in a bit of vinegar to make a thick paste. Fry this in the butter until golden. Do not burn. Add the mustard seeds and when they begin to jump, add the pork and its marinade and cook gently until meat is tender, about 40 minutes. Do not add more liquid, and keep turning the meat so that it does not scorch. This is a very dry curry.

NOTE: This dish is usually served hot, but it can also be thin-sliced and served cold.

Chapter 8

TANDOORI SPECIALTIES

The famous *tandoor*—the huge clay oven fueled to intense heat by charcoal—came to India by way of ancient Persia. At one time tandoori (food prepared in the *tandoor*) was common only in the Northern regions, but its popularity has brought this delicacy into every part of India, and lately to the Western world.

Murgh Tandoori
TANDOORI CHICKEN

It is impossible to make true tandoori chicken at home. The tandoor, a waist-high clay oven fired by an intense charcoal heat, can barbecue a whole chicken in less than 15 minutes. Nan, the classic bread cooked in the tandoor, bakes in a few minutes. There is no way we can generate such heat at home.

However, a satisfying version can be made by roasting the chicken at high heat in an oven, or, better still, by first marinating the bird and then barbecuing it on a skewer over a backyard charcoal grill, provided plenty of coals are used. Don't be surprised if your homemade chicken doesn't look precisely like that served at the Bombay Palace. It will taste wonderful all the same.

At the Bombay Palace restaurants, each order consists of half a chicken on the bone. For home skewering, it may be desirable to cut the chicken into smaller portions.

For a party, you may want to prepare Tandoori Chicken similar to the way the Bombay Palace kitchens do it. The following instructions will show you how.

PREPARING THE CHICKEN FOR THE TANDOOR

1. Skin the chicken: Using a kitchen towel or a napkin, hold the chicken's body firmly in one hand, and slip the fingers of your other hand under the skin at the neck of the bird and pull. Use a sharp knife to ease the skin off from difficult points along the way. Trim all fat and sinews, and discard.

2. Cut off wing tips and discard or save for the stock pot.

3. Lay the bird on its back, breast away from you. Place a large, very sharp knife inside the carcass and open the breast. With the chicken still on its back, make three deep gashes on each breast, and one long gash down the length of each leg. Turn the bird over and make three deep gashes on each thigh, and one on each leg. With the sharp knife or a cleaver, cut the bird in half lengthwise.

BULK MARINADE FOR TANDOORI CHICKEN, BOMBAY PALACE STYLE

FOR 4 CHICKENS. SERVES 6-8.

NOTE: This recipe can be halved.

1 pint yoghurt (500 ml)
1/2 cup white vinegar
1 1/2 tablespoons ground cumin
1 tablespoon red chili powder
1 tablespoon garam masala (p. 15)
1 tablespoon salt
2 tablespoons freshly ground black pepper

1/3 cup red color, optional (see p. 9)
1/2 cup heavy cream
1 heaping tablespoon garlic/ginger paste, or 4 garlic cloves, mashed
1 piece fresh ginger, size of walnut, minced (p. 23)
1/2 cup oil

NOTE: Color is important to this dish. If you do not wish to use the traditional orange-red coloring, try substituting ½ cup sweet Hungarian paprika and 3 tablespoons tomato paste. The color of the finished bird will not be the same but it will look appetizing.

1. Mix all ingredients well in a large pan, deep enough to hold 4 chickens.

2. Marinate the chicken halves for at least six hours and preferably overnight, turning the pieces occasionally to coat them well.

3. When ready to cook the chickens, remove them from the marinade. (The marinade may be used again; refrigerated it will keep 4 or 5 days.)

COOKING BY THE HOME OVEN METHOD

1. Preheat oven to 500°F for at least ½ hour.

2. Put the chicken in a shallow pan, breast side up. Roast until crusty, about 20 minutes. Turn over and roast 10 minutes more. The chicken should be deeply crusted but never scorched.

COOKING ON A CHARCOAL GRILL.

1. Be sure to use an abundance of charcoal and wait until the bed has acquired a grey ash. Gently blow or fan away the ash, leaving coals that glow cherry red.

2. Wipe the grill with a bit of oil so that the chicken will not stick.

3. Brush the chicken with the marinade, and sprinkle with lemon juice. Grill until chicken is golden red, about 15 minutes. Turn and grill until the second side is golden, about 10 minutes, basting once with lemon juice.

TO SERVE: Put the chicken on a large heated platter, on a bed of lettuce leaves. Decorate down the center of the platter with a series of lemon slices, cut paper-thin, alternating the lemon with paper-thin slices of white onion rings. Garnish with fresh coriander leaves and serve.

GENERAL NOTE ON COOKING CHICKEN TAN-DOORI STYLE: If you marinate overnight, the meat will become tenderized and will not take quite so long to cook as in the ordinary way.

Murgh Reshmi Kabab
CHICKEN KABABS

SERVES 4.

1 3-pound (1 1/2 kg) chicken,
   skinned, boned and cut into
   bite-sized pieces

Marinade:
1 pint yoghurt (500 ml)
1/2 cup oil
4 tablespoons white vinegar
1 tablespoon garlic/ginger
   paste, or
   3 cloves garlic, mashed
   1 piece fresh ginger, size of
     walnut, minced

1 tablespoon garam masala
1/2 teaspoon ground coriander
1/2 teaspoon ground cumin
1/2 teaspoon red chili powder
1/2 teaspoon salt
generous grinding of pepper

For Garnish
4-5 lettuce leaves
2 tablespoons chopped
   coriander leaves
juice of 1 lemon

1. Prepare chicken and prepare marinade. Coat the chicken pieces in the marinade and leave for at least 4 hours, and preferably overnight.

2. Thread chicken pieces evenly on skewers, leaving space between each piece. Grill over charcoal or under a broiler until chicken is golden on all sides, basting with marinade.

3. Place lettuce leaves on warmed serving platter and top with the chicken. Garnish with the coriander leaves. Drizzle the chicken with lemon juice before serving.

Boti Kabab Masala
TANDOORI LAMB

This dish is another favorite in the Bombay Palace restaurants, where it is prepared using the traditional tandoor. The following recipe indicates how the dish can be made from scratch.

SERVES 4.

2 pounds (1 kg) baby lamb,
   trimmed of all fat, cut into
   1-inch (3 cm) cubes

Marinade:
1 pint yoghurt (500 ml)
1/4 cup oil
4 tablespoons white vinegar
1 teaspoon garam masala
1 teaspoon garlic/ginger paste,
   or
   1 garlic clove, mashed

1 piece fresh ginger, size of
   almond, minced
1/2 teaspoon ground cumin
1/2 teaspoon red chili powder
1/2 teaspoon salt
generous grinding of fresh
   pepper

Garnish:
1 onion, sliced and separated
   into paper-thin rings
1 lemon, cut into wedges
2 tablespoons coriander leaves

1. Make gashes in the cubed meat with a sharp knife.

2. Mix all ingredients for the marinade. Rub it well into the gashes in the lamb and let the meat marinate overnight, or at least 4-6 hours. Turn the meat occasionally so that all parts are thoroughly marinated.

3. Properly, the meat should now be skewered and charcoal broiled in the intense heat of the tandoor. At home, grill the meat over a very hot charcoal bed, or do it under a broiler. Do not crowd meat when putting it on the skewers. During broiling, baste with the marinade every 5 minutes or so, and keep turning the meat.

4. When the lamb has become golden brown (about 10-15 minutes) remove from fire and place on serving platter. Distribute the onion rings over the meat, and add the garnish of coriander leaves. Arrange lemon wedges around the meat attractively and serve while hot.

NOTE: You may squeeze some fresh lemon juice over the meat just before serving.

Murgh Tikka
CHICKEN BARBECUE

1 pound (¹/₂ kg) chicken
    breasts, boned and skinned
6 ounces (180 gm) yoghurt
2 tablespoons heavy cream
2 tablespoons oil
1 tablespoon fresh-ground
    pepper
1 tablespoon garam masala

1 tablespoon garlic/ginger
    paste, or
  3 garlic cloves, mashed
  1 piece fresh ginger, size of
    walnut, minced
2 tablespoons lemon juice
3 tablespoons white vinegar
1 tablespoon orange-red color
    (optional)
¹/₂ teaspoon salt

1. Prepare chicken breasts. Cut each half-breast into 3 pieces.

2. Mix all the spices and other ingredients into the yoghurt. Add the chicken pieces and marinate for at least 2 hours, or overnight.

3. Space the chicken pieces on skewers. Broil the chicken over charcoal or under a broiler, until golden on all sides, about 3-5 minutes.

Chapter 9

FISH AND
SEAFOOD

The Indian subcontinent is surrounded by three seas: the Arabian Ocean, the Indian Ocean and the Bay of Bengal. Fish are so plentiful in the Bay of Bengal that the Bengalese, otherwise chiefly vegetarians, long ago named fish "fruit of the sea," so they could add them to their diet. The pomfret, typically used in many recipes, is a wonderfully tasty fish that, alas, only reaches our shores in a frozen state. Although pomfret would be the fish of choice for many of the recipes which follow, American sole makes a good substitute.

Jhinga Tandoori
TANDOORI PRAWNS

NOTE: To devein shrimps, use a very sharp knife to make a 1/8-inch (1/2 cm) deep slit down the back of the shrimp, from the head all the way to the tail. With the tip of the knife, extract the black vein and discard.

SERVES 4.

1 pound medium-sized
   shrimps
6 ounces (180 gm) yoghurt
juice of half a lemon
1 tablespoon oil
1 teaspoon garlic/ginger paste,
   or
   1 garlic clove, mashed
   1 piece ginger, size of
     almond, minced

1 teaspoon garam masala
1/2 teaspoon salt
generous grinding of black
   pepper
2 teaspoons orange-red color
   (optional)

1. Shell and devein the shrimps. Butterfly the shrimps by slicing them almost through lengthwise. Set aside.

2. In a bowl, mix the yoghurt and oil with all the spices and blend well. Put the shrimps into the marinade and leave them for at least 2 hours.

3. Fix the shrimp on a skewer and broil, preferably over hot charcoal, for 4-5 minutes, turning to cook evenly. Serve with rice and chutneys.

Jhinga Masala
SHRIMP MASALA

SERVES 4.

20 jumbo shrimps, peeled,
   deveined, and washed
1/4 cup oil
2 medium onions, minced
   fine, or pureed in a blender
   with a bit of water
1 tablespoon garlic/ginger
   paste, or
   3 garlic cloves, mashed
   1 piece fresh ginger, size of
   walnut, minced

Dry Masala:
1 teaspoon ground coriander
1/2 teaspoon ground cumin
1/2 teaspoon paprika
1/2 teaspoon turmeric
1/2 teaspoon ground cinnamon
1/4 teaspoon red chili powder
salt and freshly ground pepper
   to taste

2 large tomatoes, chopped fine
1/2 cup heavy cream
2 teaspoons garam masala
   (p.15–19)
4 tablespoons chopped
   coriander leaves

1. Prepare shrimp. Bring to boil enough water to cover the shrimp, add in the shrimp and boil 3 minutes. Drain and set aside, saving the water.

2. In a wok or heavy skillet, heat the oil. Saute the onions until they start to turn brown. Do not scorch. Add garlic/ginger paste and *bhoona* 2 min-

utes. Add dry masala and *bhoona* over medium-high heat 2 minutes.

3. Add tomatoes and *bhoona* until thickened to a gravy, 5-8 minutes. Stir in the cream.

6. Just before serving, garnish with the garam masala and the coriander.

Machli Ka Salan
CURRIED SALMON

SERVES 4.

2 pounds (1 kg) fresh salmon, washed well and cut into 1¹/₂-inch (4 cm) pieces

Dry Masala:
1 teaspoon (5 gms) butter
1 teaspoon turmeric
¹/₂ teaspoon red chili flakes

4 ounces (120 gm) butter (1 stick)
1 large onion, chopped fine
1 tablespoon tamarind juice (optional)

3 tablespoons water
4 ounces (120 gm) butter (1 stick)

Full Masala:
1 3-inch (8 cm) cinnamon stick, broken
1 fresh red chili, sliced thin, or 1 teaspoon red chili flakes
1 garlic clove, mashed
1 bay leaf
3 cardamom pods, crushed
2 tablespoons coriander leaves
pinch of saffron

1. Prepare fish. Mix the dry masala, and rub fish pieces into it, to coat well. Set aside for 1 hour.

2. When ready to cook, heat 4 ounces (120 gms) butter in a wok or heavy skillet and saute the onions until they begin to turn dark brown. Remove from pan and set aside. In the same pan, saute fish slices lightly on both sides. Replace the onions, and add the tamarind juice (if used), 3 tablespoons water, the second 4 ounces (120 gm) of butter, and the full masala. Simmer over low heat for 15 minutes, or until fish is almost dry. Be careful not to let fish scorch.

118

Bhoonihui Machli
FRIED SOLE

SERVES 4.

2 sole fillets, about 1 pound
  (¹/₂ kg) each, cut into 3
  pieces

Dry Masala:
1 teaspoon coriander
1 teaspoon turmeric
1 teaspoon minced onion
¹/₂ teaspoon red pepper flakes

¹/₂ teaspoon salt
pinch of freshly ground
  nutmeg

¹/₄ pound (120 gm) butter (1
  stick)
1 large onion, sliced in
  paper-thin rings, then
  halved

1. Wash fish well. Rub all the pieces of sole with the dry masala. Set aside for 1 hour.

2. In a wok or a heavy skillet, melt the butter and saute the onion slices until they begin to turn dark brown. Remove onions with slotted spoon and set aside.

3. Saute the fish on both sides until just cooked, 3-5 minutes.

4. Turn out on warmed serving platter, top with the onions and serve. This dish goes well with Indian breads and chutneys.

Machli Masala
BOMBAY FISH CURRY

SERVES 4.

2 pounds (1 kg) red snapper or
  other fresh fish fillets
1 teaspoon salt
1 lime or lemon, cut in half
oil for deep frying

1 tablespoon oil
2 onions, chopped
$1/2$ cup yoghurt
1 tablespoon garlic/ginger
  paste or:
  3 garlic cloves, mashed
  1 piece fresh ginger, size of
    walnut, minced
2 tomatoes, chopped

Dry Masala:
1 teaspoon ground coriander
$1/2$ teaspoon paprika
$1/2$ teaspoon turmeric
$1/2$ teaspoon red pepper flakes,
  or $1/2$ whole chili, minced
$1/2$ teaspoon ground cumin

chopped coriander leaves for
  garnish

1. Cut the fish into 2-inch (5 cm) cubes. Rub with lime or lemon, salt very lightly, and let marinate for $1/2$ hour. Deep-fry fish to a golden color, drain on paper towels and keep warm.

2. In a separate wok or heavy skillet saute the onions in 1 tablespoon oil over medium heat until they take on a rich color, about 10 minutes.

3. Drain any oil from the pan and add the yoghurt to the onions. Puree in food processor or blender.

4. Return the puree to the pan, and, over medium heat, stir constantly for 3 minutes.

5. Add the garlic/ginger paste and *bhoona* over medium heat for 10 minutes. When mixture is well browned (but not scorched) add the tomatoes and the dry masala. *Bhoona*, stirring constantly until thickened.

6. Put in the fish, cover, and simmer for 2 minutes.

7. Garnish with coriander leaves and serve.

Palace Fish Badami
FISH IN CREAM SAUCE, PALACE STYLE

SERVES 4.

1 pound (¹/₂ kg) delicate fish
   filets (for example, snapper,
   bass, sole)
juice of half a lemon
¹/₂ teaspoon salt
generous grinding of fresh
   pepper
¹/₃ cup (80 ml) oil
2 onions, finely chopped
1 tablespoon garlic/ginger
   paste or
   3 garlic cloves, mashed
   1 piece fresh ginger, size of
   walnut, minced

1 3-inch (8 cm) cinnamon
   stick
6 cardamom pods, crushed
4 whole cloves
4 tablespoons cashews (about
   ¹/₄ cup), ground into a paste
¹/₂ cup hot water
6 ounces (180 gm) yoghurt
4 tablespoons heavy cream
2 tablespoons chopped
   coriander leaves for garnish

1. Cut fish into 1-inch (3 cm) cubes. Put fish in a bowl and rub well with the lemon juice. Sprinkle with salt and pepper. Cover and set aside to marinate at least ¹/₂ hour or refrigerate overnight.

2. In a wok or heavy skillet, heat the oil and add the onions. Stir-fry over medium heat until golden, about 10 minutes. Stir in the garlic/ginger paste. Add the cinnamon stick, the cardamom and the cloves. Stir-fry over medium heat for 2 minutes.

3. Reduce heat slightly and add the fish pieces, very gently stirring until fish is done, about 2 minutes.

4. Add the cashew paste. Blend in the ¹/₂ cup of hot water, and bring mixture to a boil. Reduce heat and stir in the yoghurt. Simmer for 3 minutes, then pour in the cream. Remove from the stove and serve at once, garnished with the coriander leaves.

Chapter 10

VEGETARIAN SPECIALTIES AND EGG DISHES

Over the centuries, India has been known as the cradle of vegetarianism, so it is hardly surprising that vegetarian cookery holds a place of honor throughout the continent. In vegetarian and nonvegetarian households alike, vegetables are a key element of a given meal.

The delicious, hearty dishes which result from sophisticated preparation techniques and subtle spicing may pleasantly surprise those Western palates still accustomed to vegetables prepared haphazardly, almost as an afterthought.

Some of the basic preparations you will find in this chapter include vegetable curries, bhujias, bhartas, saags and koftas. Dishes based on lentils, of which there are many, will be treated separately in Chapter 13.

Kalan
SPICY BANANA

To the Western mind, a highly unusual way to treat bananas, but it is typical of the imaginative Indian combinations of fresh fruits and vegetables with spices.

SERVES 4.

3 medium-ripe bananas
1/2 cup water
1 green chili, minced
1 teaspoon turmeric
2 tablespoons oil
1 small onion, sliced thin

Full Masala:
10 peppercorns, crushed

1 teaspoon mustard seeds
1 teaspoon fenugreek seeds
1/2 teaspoon cumin seeds

2 cups yoghurt
1/4 cup unsweetened coconut
salt to taste
pinch cayenne

1. Peel bananas and slice into 1-inch (3 cm) rounds. Set aside.

2. In a wok or heavy skillet, heat 1/2 cup water and add the bananas. Sprinkle the green chili and the turmeric over the bananas and cook over low heat until the water has been absorbed. Set aside.

3. In another pan, in 1 tablespoon of oil saute the onion until it begins to turn brown. Add remaining oil and add the full masala. Stir, and when the seeds begin to jump, add the yoghurt, coconut and salt. Gently stir in the bananas and sprinkle the pinch of cayenne on top.

The dish can now be served. However, it is customary to let the dish cool for an hour or two so that all flavors are well blended, and then serve at room temperature.

Badi Rajma
RED KIDNEY BEANS

This dish can be served hot as a vegetable or a main dish, or at room temperature as an appetizer.

SERVES 4.

1 pound (¹/₂ kg) red kidney beans (If using canned beans, discard liquid, or save for another use.)
3 tablespoons butter or oil

2 onions, chopped fine
juice of 1 lemon
salt and fresh-ground pepper to taste

1. Pick over and wash beans. Soak overnight. Drain off liquid.
NOTE: If using canned beans, begin recipe at Step 3.

2. In a wok or heavy saucepan, bring beans to boil in water to cover. Partly cover with a lid and simmer 3-4 hours until tender. Stir occasionally, very gently towards the end of cooking so as not to break the beans.

3. In a wok or heavy skillet, heat the fat and saute the onions until dark brown and crisp. Gently stir in the beans, add the lemon juice and season to taste. Simmer until well heated.

4. Garnish with tardka (p. 25) if desired.

Bandh Gobhi
CABBAGE IN CREAM

SERVES 2-4.

4 tablespoons (60 gm) butter
1 head cabbage, cored and
    chopped
1 medium onion, chopped
1 teaspoon sugar
1 teaspoon black mustard
    seeds

1 teaspoon cumin seeds
1 cup raw green peas
generous grinding of fresh
    black pepper
1/3 cup heavy cream

1. In a wok or heavy skillet melt the butter over medium heat. Add the cabbage and onion and saute until wilted, about 3 minutes.

2. Add the rest of the ingredients except the cream, stirring until mixture is well blended. Stir in the cream and serve while very hot.

Masala Bandh Gobhi
SPICY CABBAGE

SERVES 4.

1 large head cabbage,
    shredded
3 tablespoons vegetable oil
1/2 teaspoon mustard seeds
1 small onion, chopped
1 fresh green chili, minced

1/4 teaspoon turmeric powder
1/4 teaspoon red chili powder
1 teaspoon salt
1/2 cup hot water
juice of 1 lime

1. Cut cabbage in quarters, cut out core in each piece and shred the cabbage.

2. In a wok or heavy skillet, heat oil over medium heat and add mustard seeds. When seeds begin to dance, add the onion and saute until translucent. Add green chili, turmeric and red chili powder, and stir for 1 minute.

3. Add cabbage, salt, and saute for 3 minutes, stirring continuously. Add 1/2 cup hot water and simmer 5 minutes.

4. Add the lime juice, mix thoroughly and serve.

Bandh Gobhi Ki Sabzi
SMOTHERED CABBAGE

SERVES 4.

*1 small head cabbage, (under
2 pounds [1 kg])
3 tablespoons butter
1 1/2 teaspoon cumin seeds
1 small onion, minced
1/4 teaspoon turmeric
1 piece fresh ginger, size of
Brazil nut, minced*

*1 large tomato, chopped
2 fresh green chilies, seeded
and minced
1/2 teaspoon salt
1 cup hot water
2 tablespoons coriander leaves
for garnish*

1. Quarter the cabbage and cut out the core from each part. Shred cabbage into 1/4 inch (3/4 cm) shreds. Set aside.

2. In a wok or heavy skillet, melt the butter over medium-high heat. Add the cumin and when it begins to dance, about 15 seconds, add the onion and immediately afterward the cabbage. Sprinkle the turmeric over the cabbage and saute, stirring until cabbage is wilted, about 5 minutes.

3. Add the ginger, tomato, and chilies and saute for another 3 minutes. Add salt plus the cup of hot water.

4. Cover and turn heat to medium-low. Simmer until all liquid has been absorbed, about 20 minutes. Check occasionally and stir so cabbage does not burn.

5. Garnish with coriander leaves and serve.

Aloo Gobhi Masala
CAULIFLOWER WITH POTATOES AND SPICES

SERVES 4-6.

1 large cauliflower, cut into
    flowerets
4 medium potatoes, peeled
1/4 cup vegetable oil
1 teaspoon cumin seeds
1 tablespoon garlic/ginger
    paste, or
    3 garlic cloves, mashed
    1 piece fresh ginger, size of
      walnut, minced

Dry Masala:
3/4 teaspoon turmeric
1/2 teaspoon red chili flakes
salt and freshly ground
    pepper to taste

3 tomatoes, chopped
1 teaspoon garam masala
    (pp. 15–19)
2 tablespoons coriander for
    garnish

1. Wash cauliflower and prepare flowerets. Slice the potatoes in half lengthwise, and then slice each potato into six parts.

2. In a wok or heavy skillet, heat the oil. Saute the cumin 1 minute until seeds begin to dance. Add garlic/ginger paste, stir and add the potatoes. *Bhoona* 3 minutes. Add the dry masala, and *bhoona* 3 minutes. Add the tomatoes. Cover and simmer 5 minutes. (For *bhoona* technique, see p. 13.)

3. Add the cauliflower and *bhoona* over high heat for 1 minute.

4. Turn heat to low. Cover and steam vegetables for 15 minutes. Uncover, and if necessary, turn heat up to "dry" vegetables.

Sprinkle on the garam masala, turn onto a warm platter and garnish with chopped coriander.

Gobhi Matar Tamatar
CAULIFLOWER WITH PEAS AND TOMATOES

SERVES 4.

1 medium cauliflower, cut
    into flowerets
2 tablespoons oil
1 small onion, chopped fine

Dry Masala:
1 teaspoon ground coriander
$^1/_2$ teaspoon turmeric
$^1/_4$ teaspoon red chili powder

3 large tomatoes, peeled and
    chopped fine
1 teaspoon salt
1 bay leaf, crumbled
1 cup fresh peas (or 1 package
    frozen)
2 tablespoons coriander leaves
    for garnish

1. Cut up cauliflower and set aside.

2. In a wok or heavy skillet, heat the oil and add the onion. Saute until onion turns golden. Add the dry masala and saute for 3 minutes. Add the flowerets and saute 3 minutes. Add tomatoes, salt, bay leaf and $^1/_4$ cup water. Add the peas. Cover and simmer a few minutes until vegetables are just tender.

3. Garnish with coriander leaves and serve.

Paneer Makhani
CHEESE CUBES IN BUTTER TOMATO SAUCE

Butter Tomato Sauce (p. 28) is one of the richest and most delicious of the major sauces used by Bombay Palace chefs. Almost any ingredients can be added to it to create an elegant, festive dish. Here we suggest paneer, the fresh Indian cheese. Use your imagination to create other dishes.

SERVES 4.

1 recipe of paneer (Indian
    cheese), deep fried (p. 27)
2 tablespoons oil

$^2/_3$ cup (160 gms) butter
    tomato sauce (p. 28)

TO ASSEMBLE THE DISH:
Place fried cheese cubes on a heated platter, cover with warmed sauce and serve at once. If you wish, garnish with fresh coriander leaves.

Bharwan Baigan
EGGPLANT STUFFED WITH KEEMA

These well-seasoned stuffed vegetables are equally good as a main dish or as vegetable accompaniment to a meat or rice dish.

SERVES 6.

2 cups leftover or freshly made keema (p. 65, 100) for stuffing
3 small eggplants, not peeled, cut in half lengthwise

oil to moisten eggplant
1 egg beaten
1 cup bread crumbs

1. Preheat oven to 500°F.

2. After slicing eggplants, carefully scoop out the meat leaving only the shell. (A grapefruit spoon is an ideal tool for this; otherwise use a sharp pointed knife.) Mince the eggplant pulp and add it to the keema, if desired. Otherwise reserve for another use.

3. Fill each half with the keema, mounding the mixture above the shell sides. Moisten the outside of the shells with oil, and moisten the top edges with beaten egg. Dribble breadcrumbs over the top of each shell.

4. Place the shells, meat side up, on a baking sheet and bake for 15 minutes. Turn off heat and leave eggplants in the oven to brown for 10 minutes more.

Bharava Hari Mirch
STUFFED GREEN PEPPER

This recipe is prepared in the same manner as the stuffed eggplants on preceding page.

SERVES 6.

4 cups leftover or freshly made
keema for stuffing
6 plump bell green peppers

1 egg beaten
1 cup bread crumbs
oil to moisten peppers

1. Preheat oven to 500°F.

2. Carefully cut off the tops of the peppers and discard seeds and interior fibers, leaving 6 hollow shells.

3. Stuff the peppers with keema until the meat mounds over the top edge of the shells. Moisten the shells with oil and moisten the edge of the shells with beaten egg. Dribble breadcrumbs over the top of each pepper.

4. Place the stuffed peppers upright on a baking sheet and bake them 15 minutes. Turn off the oven and leave them to brown for 10 minutes more.

Baigan Piaz Masala
SPICY EGGPLANT WITH ONIONS

2 eggplants, about 3 pounds
   (1¹/₂ kg), peeled and cut into
   2-inch (5 cm) cubes
4 tablespoons oil
1 teaspoon fennel seeds
1 teaspoon fenugreek seeds
2 onions, chopped coarsely
1 teaspoon ground coriander

1 teaspoon ground cumin
1 teaspoon amchoor powder
   (sour dry mango), or
   substitute 1 teaspoon lemon
   juice
¹/₄ teaspoon red chili powder
1 cup water

1. Prepare eggplants and set aside.

2. In a wok or heavy skillet heat the oil over medium-low heat. Add the fennel and fenugreek seeds. When they start to change color in a few seconds, quickly add the onions and eggplant cubes. Lower the heat and *bhoona* for 15 minutes. Do not let the mixture scorch. Add a bit of water if necessary. Add the coriander, cumin, amchoor and red chili powder.

3. Add 1 cup water, cover, and simmer gently until eggplant is tender, about 15 minutes. Check for seasoning. You might want to make the dish tarter or hotter by adding more amchoor or red chili powder.

Baigan Bharta
SPICED EGGPLANT PUREE

SERVES 4-6.

1 large eggplant, about 2
   pounds (1 kg), peeled and
   cut into 2-inch (5 cm) cubes
1/2 cup oil
2 onions, coarsely chopped
4 tomatoes, coarsely chopped
juice of 1/2 lime
salt and freshly ground pepper
   to taste

Dry Masala:
1 teaspoon paprika
1/2 teaspoon red chili powder
1/2 teaspoon turmeric
1 teaspoon garam masala

2 tablespoons coriander leaves
   for garnish

1. Prepare eggplant and set aside.

2. In a wok or heavy skillet, heat oil just short of smoking. *Bhoona* eggplant cubes until soft, 7-10 minutes. Remove and set aside. To the oil add the onions, and cook until they become translucent. Add the tomatoes, the lime juice, salt and pepper, and the dry masala.

3. Return eggplant to pan and *bhoona* over medium heat, mashing the eggplant as you stir. *Bhoona* until eggplant is tender, about 3-5 minutes. You will end up with a coarse-textured puree.

4. Turn out on warmed serving platter and sprinkle with the Garam Masala. Garnish with the coriander leaves and serve.

Bhooni Bhindi
CRISP-FRIED OKRA

This makes a delightful garnish for many dishes, especially for dry minced lamb or beef.

SERVES 2-4 AS A GARNISH.

2 pounds (1 kg) fresh okra

3/4 cup oil

1. Wash okra under cold running water, and wipe dry. Cut off both ends and slice into very thin rounds.

2. In a wok or heavy skillet, heat the oil just to the smoking point. Add the okra in a single layer. Let sizzle for 1 minute, then reduce heat to medium. Turn and toss the okra until crisply brown, about 20 minutes. Remove with slotted spoon and drain on paper towels.

Bhindi Masala
SPICED OKRA WITH ONIONS

Westerners sometimes dislike okra because of its rather gummy taste. This recipe turns okra into a marvelous surprise.

NOTE: The smaller okra, the better the taste.

SERVES 4-6.

1 pound (¹/₂ kg) okra
2 onions, thinly sliced
2 tomatoes, chopped
¹/₄ cup oil
³/₄ teaspoon paprika
1 teaspoon amchoor powder
    (or substitute fresh lemon
    juice)

¹/₂ teaspoon turmeric
salt and freshly ground pepper
    to taste
1 teaspoon garam masala
2 tablespoons chopped
    coriander leaves for garnish

1. Wash okra under running water and slice off the ends. Cut each in half. Set aside. Prepare onions and tomatoes. Set aside.

2. In a wok or heavy skillet heat the oil and saute onions until translucent.

3. Add all spices except the garam masala and stir-fry 2 minutes. Add the tomatoes and *bhoona* 1 minute. Add the okra and stir-fry 2 minutes. Cover and steam over medium heat until tender, about 12-15 minutes.

4. Spoon the okra onto a warm serving plate and sprinkle with the garam masala. Garnish with the coriander and serve while hot.

Piaz Bhujia
SPICY ONION TANGLES

These crunchy tidbits always leave one wanting to taste "just one more." Because of the loose distribution of the whole spices, each bite produces a different delicious "explosion" of tastes. Ideal as an accompaniment for cocktails.

SERVES 6.

1 small eggplant, not peeled, sliced into matchsticks
1 large potato, scrubbed but not peeled, sliced into matchsticks
1 large onion, sliced thin, cut into half-rings and separated
1/4 pound (120 gm) besan (chick-pea flour)
2 ounces (60 gm) white flour
1/4 teaspoon baking soda
1 teaspoon salt

1 teaspoon whole coriander seeds
1 teaspoon whole cumin seeds
1/2 teaspoon red chili pepper flakes
1/2 teaspoon fresh-ground pepper
1 teaspoon cumin powder
1 teaspoon coriander powder
1 teaspoon ground red chili
enough oil to cover bottom of a pan to about 1/2 inch

1. Prepare the eggplant, potato and onion and mix them well together.

2. On a large plate or in a shallow bowl, mix the two flours and the baking soda and salt with all the spices.

3. Add the vegetables to the flour, mixing with your hands to coat them well. Dribble on a bit of water, about 1/4 cup, and again using your hands, blend the bhujia into a loose mass. NOTE: This mix should be a bit sticky, but almost dry—do not make a batter.

4. In a wok or heavy pot, heat the oil and turn flame to medium-high. Dribble in the vegetable mixture a small handful at a time. The coating of spices and flour will bind the vegetables into a loose patty. Turn the bhujia cluster several times and cook until it is a dark brown but not scorched, about 5-10 minutes. Set each cluster on paper towels to drain. Serve while still hot and crisp.

NOTE: The bhujia can be made ahead of time, well-drained of oil, and then crisped by being put into a preheated 350°F oven for half an hour.

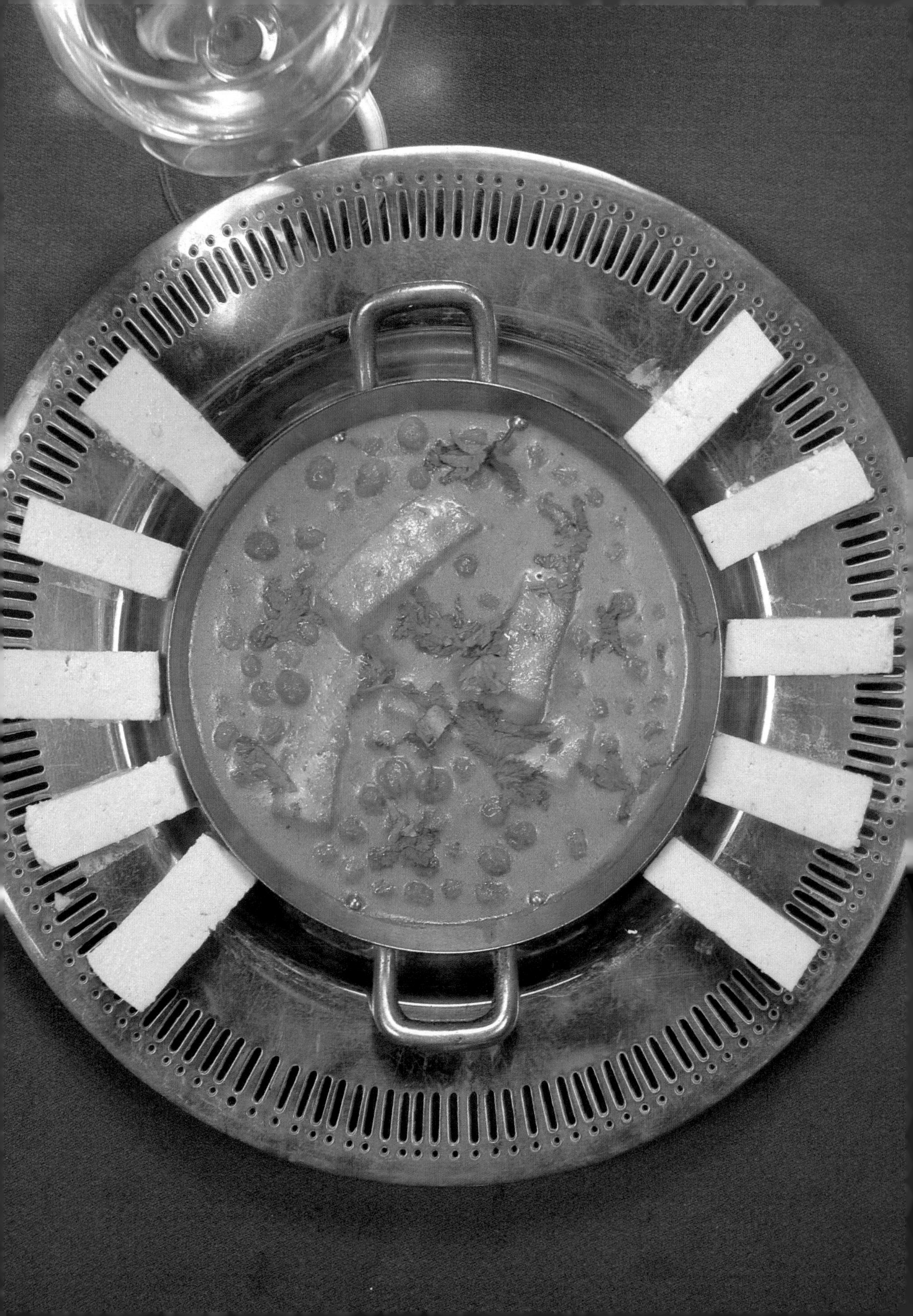

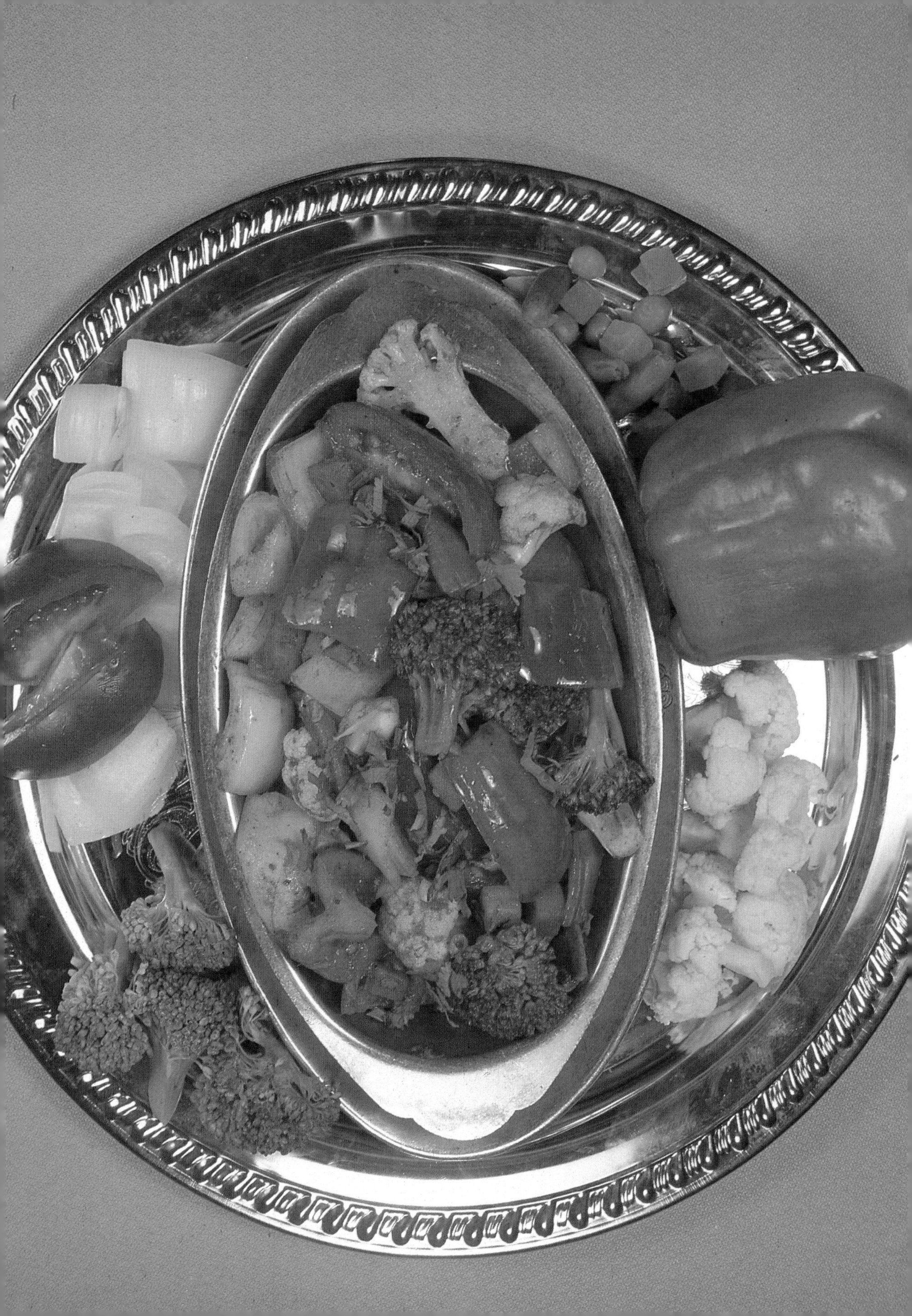

Matar Paneer
PEAS AND CHEESE CUBES

SERVES 4-6.

6 paneer chunks (p. 27) about
   1¹/₂ × 1 × ¹/₂ inch each
   (4 × 3 × 1¹/₂ cm)
¹/₄ cup oil
1 medium onion, chopped fine
1 tablespoon garlic/ginger
   paste, or
   3 garlic cloves, mashed
   1 piece fresh ginger, size of
     walnut, minced
   1 large tomato, chopped

Dry Masala:
¹/₂ teaspoon ground coriander

¹/₄ teaspoon ground cumin
¹/₄ teaspoon red chili powder
¹/₄ teaspoon turmeric
¹/₂ teaspoon garam masala

¹/₄ cup water
3 cups fresh shelled green
   peas (or substitute 2
   packages frozen)
1 tablespoon cashew nuts,
   ground to a paste with a
   bit of water
salt and freshly ground
   pepper to taste

1. Prepare the cheese chunks, and in a wok or heavy skillet fry them in hot oil until golden. Remove with slotted spoon and set aside to drain on a paper towel.

2. In the remaining oil saute the chopped onion until it begins to turn brown. Do not scorch. Add the garlic/ ginger paste and *bhoona* 2 minutes. Add the chopped tomato and *bhoona*

5 minutes to achieve a thick gravy. Add the dry masala and *bhoona* 3 minutes more. (NOTE: If the sauce is lumpy at this stage, puree it in a blender and continue).

3. Add ¹/₄ cup water, then stir in the peas. Add the paneer cubes and *bhoona* 2 minutes. Stir in the cashew paste, add salt, pepper; serve at once.

Saag Paneer
SPINACH WITH CHEESE SQUARES

SERVES 4.

2 pounds (1 kg) fresh spinach,
  cleaned well
3 tablespoons oil
3 onions, chopped fine
3 tomatoes, chopped fine
1 tablespoon garlic/ginger
  paste, or
  3 garlic cloves, mashed
  1 piece fresh ginger, size of
    walnut, minced

Dry Masala:
$1/2$ teaspoon ground cumin
$1/2$ teaspoon ground coriander
$1/2$ teaspoon turmeric
$1/2$ teaspoon paprika
$1/2$ teaspoon fenugreek leaves,
  crushed
$1/4$ teaspoon red chili powder

$1/2$ cup yoghurt
  1 recipe fried paneer squares
  $1/3$ cup heavy cream

1. Boil the spinach 2 minutes. Drain, chop, and set aside.

2. In a wok or heavy skillet heat 2 tablespoons oil and saute onions until they turn golden. Add the tomatoes, the garlic/ginger paste, and the dry masala. *Bhoona* to make a thick paste, stirring constantly. Add the spinach and stir-fry until well mixed, about 2 minutes. Add the yoghurt and simmer 2 minutes. Add the fried paneer squares and *bhoona* 3 minutes. Add the heavy cream, and stir until sauce thickens, about 3 minutes. Serve hot.

Saag Aloo
SPINACH WITH POTATOES

Spinach, a very popular vegetable in India, is grown in several different varieties. This is a fairly simple but delicious way of cooking spinach. The addition of potatoes is a typical Indian touch.

SERVES 4.

2 pounds fresh spinach (1 kg)
1 teaspoon salt
4 tablespoons (60 gm) butter
2 onions, sliced and separated
   into paper-thin rings
1 piece fresh ginger, size of
   walnut, minced

2 green chilies, seeded and
   chopped fine
1 teaspoon turmeric
1 pound (¹/₂ kg) potatoes,
   peeled and cut into thick
   slices (optional)

1. Wash spinach thoroughly and place it with the salt in a wok or large saucepan, with only the water that clings to the leaves. Cook over high heat, stirring constantly, for 1 minute. Reduce heat to medium and cook for 3 minutes, stirring occasionally. Drain the spinach and remove it to a board. Chop it coarsely.

2. In a wok or heavy skillet heat the butter and add the onions, ginger and chilies. Stir-fry until onions are golden. Stir in the turmeric.

3. Add the potatoes, if desired, reduce heat to low, cover the pan and simmer until potatoes are just tender, about 20 minutes.

4. Add the spinach, raise heat to medium and stir until most of the moisture has evaporated, about 3 minutes.

Shalgam Rasa
TURNIPS IN CURRY SAUCE

Westerners are apt to think of the turnip as a lowly vegetable.
Indian cooks give it the sophisticated treatment it deserves.

SERVES 4-6.

2 pounds (1 kg) young turnips
   (not rutabagas!), cleaned
   and cut into *1/2*-inch (1 cm)
   cubes
1/4 cup oil

Full Masala
1 teaspoon coriander seeds
1 teaspoon cumin seeds

1 cup onion sauce (p. 34)

Dry Masala:
1/2 teaspoon ground coriander
1/2 teaspoon ground cumin
1/2 teaspoon garam masala
1/2 teaspoon paprika
1/2 teaspoon turmeric
1/4 teaspoon red chili powder

3 tablespoons yoghurt
1 1/2 cups water
3 ounces heavy cream
salt and freshly ground pepper
   to taste
2 tablespoons chopped
   coriander leaves for garnish

1. Prepare turnips and set aside.

2. In a wok or heavy skillet, heat the oil. Add the full masala and brown the seeds, about 5 seconds. Add the onion sauce and *bhoona* 3 minutes over high heat. Turn heat to medium and add the dry masala and the salt and pepper. *Bhoona* 5 minutes.

3. Add the diced turnips. *Bhoona* over medium heat for 10 minutes, being careful not to let the turnips scorch.

4. Add the yoghurt and simmer for 2 minutes. Add 1 1/2 cups water, cover, and simmer for 10 minutes more, or until the gravy has become very thick.

5. Stir in the heavy cream, add the salt, pepper and coriander leaves, cover, and simmer 10 minutes.

Bhujia
SPICY HOT VEGETABLES

This recipe is typical of the unusual way that Indian cuisine combines vegetables. Bhujia is served as a side dish to a curry; it is not the usual fried vegetable fritter identified by the same name.

SERVES 4.

3 medium potatoes, cut into
  1-inch (3 cm) dice
1 eggplant, cut in 1-inch (3
  cm) dice
1 tablespoon oil
1 small onion, chopped
1 teaspoon salt
1 thin slice fresh ginger,
  thickness of a coin, minced

$1^1/_2$ teaspoon powdered
  mustard
1 dried red chili, seeds
  removed, crumbled fine
$^1/_2$ teaspoon turmeric
1 cup water

1. Prepare potatoes and eggplant and set aside.

2. In a wok or heavy skillet, heat the oil, add the onion and saute until it is just slightly browned. Add the vegetables and all the other ingredients. Over medium-high heat stir constantly until vegetables are golden brown.

3. Add 1 cup of water, cover, and simmer until vegetables are tender and all liquid is absorbed, about 15 minutes. The bhujia must be dry.

Vegetable Jalfrasie
MIXED VEGETABLES

While this recipe is traditional, you may substitute any vegetables of your choice, following the same techniques.

SERVES 4.

1 large onion, chopped
  coarsely
2 bell peppers, seeded and cut
  into 1-inch (3 cm) cubes
2 large tomatoes, cut into
  1-inch (3 cm) cubes
1/2 pound (240 gm) broccoli,
  cut into 1-inch pieces (3 cm)
1/2 pound (240 gm) cauliflower,
  cut into 1-inch (3 cm) cubes
4 tablespoons (60 gm) butter
  (1/2 stick)

1 teaspoon red chili powder
  (or more to taste)
1/2 teaspoons turmeric
1 tablespoon garlic/ginger
  paste, or
  3 garlic cloves, mashed
  1 piece fresh ginger, size of
  walnut, minced
2 tablespoons white vinegar
2 tablespoons tomato puree
salt and freshly ground pepper
  to taste

1. Prepare vegetables.

2. In a wok or heavy skillet, melt the butter and add onion. When onion becomes translucent, add all remaining vegetables and stir-fry for about 5 minutes over medium heat.

3. Add the spices with the vinegar. Stir in the tomato puree. Simmer 5 minutes. Season to taste with salt and fresh-ground pepper.

Navarattan Curry
NINE VEGETABLE CURRY

This is a jewel-like fantasy of vegetables. In fact, the word *navarattan* translates as "diamonds." The nine vegetables are cut into diamond shapes adding visual elegance to the dish.

SERVES 4-6.

4 ounces (120 gm) each of the
  following vegetables,
  all cut into diamond shapes
  of the same size:
    Broccoli
    Bell Pepper, green or red
    Carrots
    Cauliflower buds
    Green beans
1 large potato, peeled and cut
  into small cubes (or
  diamonds, if you have the
  patience)
2 tablespoons (30 gm) butter
1 large onion, minced
2 garlic cloves, minced
2 tomatoes, chopped
2 tablespoons yoghurt

Dry Masala:
$1/2$ teaspoon ground
  cardamom
$1/2$ teaspoon ground coriander
$1/2$ teaspoon ground ginger
$1/2$ teaspoon red chili powder
$1/2$ teaspoon turmeric

$1/4$ cup water
$1/2$ cup heavy cream
4 ounces (120 gm) fresh green
  peas
4 ounces canned fruit cup
$1/4$ cup raisins
12 slivered blanched almonds
  for garnish

1. Parboil the vegetables (except onions and peas) separately until crisp-tender, in lightly salted water.

NOTE: You can cook them all in one pot provided you start with the potatoes for 2 minutes, then add the cauliflower, broccoli, then a minute or two later, the carrots and green beans, and finally the bell pepper, so that all these vegetables are barely cooked and firm at the same time. Drain and set aside.

2. In a wok or heavy skillet, melt the butter and add onions and garlic. Saute until translucent. Add the tomatoes, yoghurt and the dry masala and simmer for 5 minutes. Add the parboiled vegetables and simmer for another 5 minutes, then add $1/4$ cup water. Cover and simmer 10 minutes. Add the cream and the fresh peas, stirring gently to blend. Remove a few cherries from the canned fruit, for the garnish, and gently blend in the rest of the fruit.

3. Just before serving, top with the raisins and the almonds, and decorate with the cherries.

Malai Kofta
CREAMED VEGETABLE BALLS

These vegetable balls (koftas) can be served "dry" as a cocktail snack, or with the cream onion gravy as a main dish.

SERVES 4-6.

Vegetable Balls:
1 pound (¹/₂ kg) potatoes
1 large carrot, grated and
 squeezed dry
5 ounces (150 gm) fresh
 paneer, grated (Indian
 cheese p. 27)
1 tablespoon cornstarch
salt and freshly ground pepper
 to taste
¹/₄ cup blanched almonds,
 chopped fine
¹/₄ cup raisins
juice of 1 fresh lemon
 (optional)

oil for deep frying

Onion Gravy:
(Makes about 1 cup)
1 cup onions, coarsely
 chopped

2 ounces (60 gm) butter (¹/₄
 stick)

Dry Masala:
2 teaspoons paprika
¹/₂ teaspoon ground cumin
 seeds
¹/₂ teaspoon ground coriander
¹/₂ teaspoon turmeric
¹/₂ teaspoon red chili powder

1 cup water (or less)
¹/₄ teaspoon salt
1 tomato, chopped fine

4 large cashew nuts
¹/₄ cup heavy cream

Garnish:
2 tablespoon chopped
 coriander

MAKING THE VEGETABLE BALLS:

1. Peel and cut potatoes in quarters and boil for 15 minutes until tender. Drain and mash.

2. Meanwhile prepare the carrot.

3. Mix the cheese, cornstarch, salt and pepper, almonds, raisins and lemon juice together, blending well.

Shape into fat thumb-shaped cylinders.

4. Heat oil to smoking point and deep-fry vegetable balls until golden brown, about 3 or 4 minutes. Drain on paper towels. Sprinkle with lemon juice and serve hot as a snack.

MAKING THE ONION GRAVY:

1. Put onions into blender with a bit of water and puree.

2. In a wok or heavy skillet, heat the butter and add the onions. Cook for about 20 minutes over medium heat, stirring constantly, to dry the onions. Do not let them burn. Add the dry masala and stir for 3 minutes. Add enough water to make a thick gravy, about 1 cup. Add the salt and the tomato.

3. In a blender puree the cashews with a bit of water to make a paste. Stir the nut paste into the sauce and simmer 10 minutes. Stir in the heavy cream.

TO ASSEMBLE AS A MAIN DISH:

Put the vegetable balls on a warmed serving platter and cover with gravy.

Garnish with coriander leaves and serve hot.

Aloo Bhaji
POTATO APPETIZER

This deliciously tangy dish can be served either as a side dish to a meal, as an appetizer, or by itself as a snack.

SERVES 4 AS A SIDE DISH; 6-8 AS A SNACK.

5 potatoes
1 medium onion, chopped
2 fresh green chilies, chopped
1 ripe tomato, chopped
1 piece fresh ginger, size of
  walnut, minced
1/2 cup oil
1 tablespoon cumin seeds
2 tablespoons yoghurt

1 rounded teaspoon turmeric
1 tomato, chopped
generous grinding of fresh
  pepper
1/2 teaspoon salt
1 tablespoon garam masala
2 tablespoons chopped
  coriander leaves

1. Boil the potatoes 15 minutes. Cool, peel and cut into 1-inch (3 cm) cubes. Set aside.

2. In a wok or heavy skillet heat the oil and add the chopped onions and chilies, along with the ginger and the cumin seeds. When the onions just begin to become translucent, add the yoghurt, the turmeric and the chopped tomato. Stir in the salt and pepper.

3. Add the potatoes to the mixture and cook until potatoes are warmed through, about 3 minutes. Add the garam masala and the coriander leaves and gently stir for another 2 minutes. Serve hot.

Akoori
SCRAMBLED EGGS, PARSI STYLE

SERVES 4.

6 large eggs
4 tablespoons milk
1/2 teaspoon salt
generous grinding of black
  pepper
2 tablespoons (30 gm) butter
6 scallions, chopped fine
3 fresh green chilies, seeded
  and minced

1 piece fresh ginger, size of
  walnut, minced
2 teaspoons ground turmeric
1 tomato, diced small
1/2 teaspoon ground cumin
1 small tomato cut in wedges
  for garnish
2 tablespoons fresh coriander
  leaves for garnish

1. Beat eggs, add the milk, salt and pepper.

2. In a wok or large skillet melt the butter and cook the scallions, chilies and ginger until onions are translucent. Add coriander and turmeric and blend well. Add beaten eggs, diced tomato and the cumin. Holding a fork parallel to the bottom of the pan, stir and lift from the bottom until the eggs are cooked to your taste. Turn onto a heated platter, garnish with tomato wedges and coriander leaves and serve while very hot, accompanied by hot buttered toast or parathas.

Kitchuri Unda
SCRAMBLED EGGS, INDIAN STYLE

SERVES 2.

1/2 onion, minced
1 tomato, diced
2 tablespoons butter
3 tablespoons chopped
  coriander leaves

1 green chili, sliced very thin
4 eggs
salt and freshly ground pepper
  to taste

1. Prepare the vegetables. Melt the butter in a skillet over medium heat. Add onions and saute until they begin to turn golden. Add the tomato, coriander and chili. Stir 3 minutes, until tomato begins to soften.

2. Meanwhile, beat the eggs. Pour them into the skillet and season with salt and pepper. Holding a fork parallel to the bottom of the skillet, stir gently from bottom of pan until eggs are cooked to your taste. Serve with hot buttered toast or parathas.

Nargisi Kofta
EGGS IN MEATBALLS

These are named for their resemblance to yellow and white narcissus (*nargisi*) blossoms. Western cooks may recognize this dish as an exotic version of "Scotch Eggs". This recipe may seem complicated, but the results are stunning.

SERVES 6.

Meatballs:
6 eggs
1 pound (¹/₂ kg) lamb or beef,
   ground fine
1 onion, minced
1 tablespoon garlic/ginger
   paste, or
   3 garlic cloves, mashed
   1 piece fresh ginger, size of
      walnut, minced
1 fresh green chili, minced
1 teaspoon salt

Dry Masala:
¹/₂ teaspoon ground cumin
¹/₂ teaspoon ground coriander
¹/₂ teaspoon turmeric
¹/₂ teaspoon red chili flakes
¹/₂ teaspoon paprika

¹/₂ cup water
¹/₂ tablespoon besan
   (chick-pea flour)
2 tablespoons yoghurt
1 egg, beaten with 1
   tablespoon water
oil for frying, about 3
   tablespoons

Curry Sauce:
1 tablespoon (15 gm) butter
1 onion, chopped fine
2 tablespoons garlic/ginger
   paste, or
   6 garlic cloves, mashed
   1 piece fresh ginger, size of
      Brazil nut, minced

Full Masala:
1 3-inch (8 cm) cinnamon
   stick
2 black cardamoms, crushed
2 green cardamom pods,
   crushed
4 cloves
¹/₂ teaspoon cumin seeds
¹/₂ teaspoon coriander seeds
2 dried red chili pods, crushed
2 bay leaves, crumbled

2 large ripe tomatoes, diced
   small
1 cup yoghurt
¹/₂ cup hot water

Garnish:
2 tablespoons chopped
   coriander leaves

146

1. Put 6 whole eggs in a pan of cold water and bring slowly to a boil. Turn eggs occasionally during the first 5 minutes, to center the yolks. When the water boils, turn heat to a simmer and cook for 10 minutes. Cool and peel the eggs and set aside.

2. In a wok or heavy skillet put the ground meat, the minced onion, the garlic/ginger paste, the green chili, the salt and the dry masala. Add 1/2 cup water, stir well, bring to a boil, then cover and simmer 15 minutes until meat is cooked. Stir in the chick-pea flour and *bhoona* until all liquid is absorbed. Cool the mixture.

3. Knead the meat until smooth, adding a bit of yoghurt, if necessary. Divide into 6 equal portions, and mould each one around a hardboiled egg.

4. Beat the additional egg and the tablespoon of water. Dip the meatballs in the beaten egg and fry in hot oil turning until golden brown. Drain on paper towels and keep warm. Meanwhile make the curry sauce.

5. CURRY SAUCE: Heat 1 tablespoon butter and saute onion until translucent. Add garlic/ginger paste and stir until onion turns golden. Do not burn. Add the full masala, stir well, then add the tomatoes. Cover and simmer for 15 minutes, or until the mixture is a pulp, stirring occasionally. Mix the yoghurt with the hot water and stir into the mixture. *Bhoona* until the mixture becomes thick, stirring to avoid scorching.

6. Add the meatballs and heat them through. Slice each meatball in half and place 4 halves on each plate, alternating the yolk and meat sides. Dribble any leftover sauce over them, garnish with coriander leaves, and serve.

Chapter 11

RICE DISHES

Rice is a staple food for half of the world's population, and is essential to much of Indian cooking. *Basmati* rice, as we have noted (p. 10) is one of the finest rices on earth, and without its special fragrance and texture, some Indian dishes cannot be considered properly made.

While plain steamed rice is often part of an ordinary meal, rice is more often used as the basis of a pulao or a biryani, which are complex and zestful rice, meat and vegetable combinations. For a pulao, basmati rice is generally sauteed in butter or oil until translucent, then cooked with broth and a mixture of nuts and vegetables or meats, or a combination of these. Biryanis are the most complicated of Indian rice dishes, these being special pilafs that are rich with meat, nuts and vegetables, and flavored with generous amounts of butter and colored by precious saffron. The Bombay Palace kitchens are famous for their regal rice dishes.

Although the Indian breads of the North are among the world's most delicious, India as a whole is a rice-eating nation. Even in Moghlai cooking, rice is given special, almost reverent, treatment. While many kinds of rice are used, the most popular is long-grain, patna. The most celebrated rice of all is basmati, which, along with Persian rice, is considered to be the world's finest. Basmati has a beautiful perfume, and there is a saying in India that when one smells basmati cooking from a house, it signifies that special guests are coming for dinner.

Basmati rice must be cooked with more care than ordinary rice. However, the procedure is simple: First the dry rice must be picked over and cleaned to make sure that no broken grains or foreign materials are present. Then the rice is washed in cold running water in a colander until the water loses its milkiness and begins to run clear. Finally, unlike other long-grain rice, basmati rice is best when it is covered with cold water and allowed to soak for 15 minutes to half an hour before being cooked.

If you do not use basmati rice, use only a good quality of long-grained rice for all these recipes. And no matter what kind of rice is used, just before serving, fluff the rice carefully, lifting the rice gently from the bottom of the pot. (Always use a fork for this operation, to avoid breaking the delicate grains of rice.)

PLAIN BOILED OR STEAMED RICE is a daily favorite.

A *KITCHURI* (a word that means 'scrambled') can be a mixture of rice and dal.

PULAO is a dish where rice is first fried then mixed with meat or vegetables.

BIRYANI is an elaborate pulao, where exotic spices such as saffron are used, and the rice layered with richly spiced meats and vegetables of various sorts.

HOW MUCH TO PREPARE:

How much rice to make for a meal is a quite personal matter. An Indian family would undoubtedly eat considerably more rice than an American one. The method on the next page should be sufficient for an American group of 4 or 6. Follow these foolproof instructions exactly and you will always make perfect rice.

Basmati Rice

As we have pointed out, basmati is a very special rice and requires special attention to bring out its wonderful fragrance to the full. It is also a delicate rice and must always be handled gently.

SERVES 4-6.

2 cups basmati rice
1 1/2 cups water, approximately

1 tablespoon (15 gm) butter
1/4 teaspoon salt

1. Spread the basmati on a large flat plate and clean it of all impurities. Wash thoroughly by putting rice in a colander and then under a faucet until the water runs clear.

2. Put the basmati in a bowl and cover well with water. Let soak for 15 minutes to 1/2 hour. Drain rice and then proceed with recipe.

NOTE

TO SUBSTITUTE AMERICAN LONG-GRAIN RICE: American rice has generally been cleaned. It has also been treated to retain some of its vitamins. Therefore, do NOT wash or soak ordinary long-grain rice. Instead, simply measure it from the package and proceed with recipe, but use 3 cups of water to the 2 cups of rice.

3. Melt the butter in a heavy-bottomed pot (or a Corning ware type ceramic pot) that has a very tight-fitting lid. If the lid does not fit tightly, cover the pot with a cloth napkin before putting on the lid. Add the rice and very gently stir to coat with the butter.

4. Regardless of the amount of rice in the pot add water to cover an additional 1 inch (3 cm). Add the salt.

5. Bring the rice to a full boil and wait until tiny "wells" begin to appear in the surface. Gently stir, then tightly cover the pot and turn heat as low as possible. Let steam for 15 minutes.

6. Turn off heat and let rice continue to steam another 5 minutes. DO NOT REMOVE COVER AT ANY TIME DURING THE STEAMING PERIOD. After the rice has "rested", remove the lid and—using a fork—gently lift rice from the bottom to fluff it.

Rice prepared in this manner, kept covered, will stay warm 1/2 hour or more.

Korma Chawal
CURRIED RICE

SERVES 4-6.

4 tablespoons (60 gm) butter
  (¹/2 stick)
2 onions, sliced thin
1 piece fresh ginger, size of
  walnut, minced
3 fresh green chilies, seeded
  and quartered
1 bay leaf
2 cups fresh vegetables in
  season, diced, or substitute
  2 packages of frozen mixed
  vegetables if absolutely
  necessary
2 cups long-grain rice

Dry Masala:
2 teaspoons salt
2 teaspoons ground coriander
1¹/2 teaspoons ground cumin
1 teaspoon garam masala
  (optional)
¹/2 teaspoon red chili powder
¹/2 teaspoon turmeric

3 cups chicken stock
2 tablespoons coriander leaves
  for garnish

1. In a wok or heavy skillet, heat the butter, and add the onions. Stir-fry slowly until onions begin to turn brown, but are not scorched. Add the ginger, the chilies, bay leaf and vegetables and stir-fry 2 minutes. Add the rice and stir constantly until the rice begins to glisten, about 2 minutes.

2. Stir in the dry masala. Add the stock and bring to full boil. Cover and simmer for 15 minutes.

3. Remove pot from heat and let stand 10 minutes, being sure not to lift the cover. Then gently fluff rice with a fork, lifting from the bottom.

4. Garnish with coriander leaves and serve.

Vangi Barta
EGGPLANT AND RICE

SERVES 4-6.

4 cups hot steamed rice
1 large eggplant, peeled and
   cut in small dice
3 tablespoons oil

Dry Masala:
1 tablespoon ground coriander
1 teaspoon ground cumin
1 teaspoon mustard seeds,
   crushed

$^1/_4$ teaspoon turmeric
$^1/_4$ teaspoon red chili powder
generous pinch of asafetida (or
   $^1/_2$ onion minced)

1 teaspoon salt
juice of $^1/_2$ lime
$^1/_4$ cup water

1. Steam 2 cups raw rice (p. 150). Set aside. Prepare the eggplant.

2. In a wok or heavy skillet, heat the oil and saute the dry masala over high heat for 2 minutes, stirring constantly. Add diced eggplant and saute over medium-high heat 5 minutes. Add a bit more oil during cooking if necessary.

3. Sprinkle with the salt and the lime juice. Add $^1/_4$ cup water. *Bhoona* until water has evaporated and eggplant is tender, 7-10 minutes. Very gently stir in cooked rice with a fork, being careful not to mash the eggplant. Serve at once.

Matar Pulao
RICE PILAF WITH FRESH PEAS

SERVES 4.

1½ cup basmati rice (no
  substitute)
2 tablespoons butter (30 gm)

Full Masala:
1 cinnamon stick 2 inches
  long (5 cm)

2 cardamom pods, crushed
1 teaspoon cumin seeds

1 teaspoon salt
2½ cups hot water
1½ cups fresh green peas

1. First pick over, then wash basmati rice in a colander under the faucet until the water runs clear. Set rice aside to soak in water to cover at least 15 minutes; drain when ready to use.

2. In a wok or heavy skillet with a tight-fitting lid, melt the butter over medium heat and add the full masala, saute until the seeds begin to hop around, about 1 minute. Add the drained rice and stir-fry for about 3 minutes, until rice is well-coated with butter and begins to glisten. Add the salt and 2½ cups of hot water, and bring to boil.

3. Cover tightly and simmer on lowest heat for a total of 15 minutes. After 10 minutes, quickly but gently stir in the peas, re-cover and steam 3 minutes longer. When rice is done, turn off the heat and let rice steam for another 5 minutes. Do not lift lid during steaming period. Just before serving, gently fluff rice, using a fork so as not to break rice grains.

Narial Chawal
COCONUT RICE

SERVES 4.

1½ cups grated unsweetened
   coconut
4 cups water
4 tablespoons (60 gm) butter
   (½ stick)

Full Masala:
1 garlic clove, mashed
4 whole cloves
2 whole cardamoms
1 1-inch (3 cm) stick
   cinnamon

½ cup cashews, coarsely
   chopped
¼ green pepper, minced
¼ teaspoon red chili powder

1 onion, sliced thin
2 cups rice
1 teaspoon salt
1 large ripe tomato coarsely
   chopped
salt and fresh-ground pepper
   to taste

1. In a small pot bring 1 cup of coconut to boil in 4 cups of water. Remove from heat and let cool for 15 minutes. Strain and press out all moisture, reserving the liquid for cooking the rice. Discard coconut.

2. Mix all the ingredients for the full masala.

3. In a wok or heavy skillet with a tight-fitting lid, melt the butter and saute the onion until translucent.

Add the full masala and saute for 3 minutes, stirring constantly. Add the rice and stir until rice is well coated, about 3 minutes.

4. Meanwhile bring the reserved coconut liquid to a boil, add to the rice, at the same time adding the tomato and the salt, along with the remaining ½ cup of fresh coconut. Stir gently and cover tightly. Simmer at lowest heat until rice is done, 15 minutes.

Til Chawal
SESAME RICE

SERVES 4.

4 cups of hot, cooked rice (p. 150)
4 tablespoons butter (¹/₂ stick, 60 gm)
2 tablespoons cashews

4 tablespoons sesame seeds
1 bay leaf, crumbled
¹/₂ teaspoon red chili powder
1 teaspoon salt
juice of ¹/₂ lime

1. While the rice is being steamed, melt 1 tablespoon of butter in a wok or heavy skillet, and saute the cashews to a golden brown over low heat. Remove cashews and set aside.

2. Add the remaining butter and saute the sesame seeds, bay leaf and red chili powder until the seeds turn golden and start to hop in the pan.

3. Combine the cashew nuts and the sesame seed mixture, add the salt, and very gently stir everything into the rice, using a fork.

4. Sprinkle with lime juice and serve.

Murgh Pulao
CHICKEN WITH SPICED RICE

This elegant party dish is not as complicated as its lengthy recipe might suggest. The trick is to organize everything in advance, a hint that makes all Indian cooking easier. Because of the cardamoms, almonds and the saffron, this dish is not inexpensive to serve, but when you do your guests will be dining like royalty. For this regal dish be sure to use basmati rice. It deserves it.

SERVES 4-6.

Marinade:
Prepare the day before and refrigerate overnight to mellow:
1 large or two small tomatoes, peeled and quartered
juice of 1 large lemon
4 garlic cloves, mashed
2 dried chilies, crumbled
1 rounded teaspoon cumin seeds
1 piece fresh ginger, size of Brazil nut, minced
1 3-inch (8 cm) cinnamon stick, broken in pieces
4 cardamom pods, crushed
6 peppercorns
4 cloves

1¹/₂ cups yoghurt
2 tablespoons oil

Pulao:
12 chicken legs and thighs, skinned and cut into 24 pieces (deboned if preferred)
4 tablespoons (60 gm) butter (¹/₂ stick)

4 large onions, sliced into paper-thin rings
¹/₂ cup blanched almonds, sliced
4 cardamom pods, crushed
2 bay leaves

2 cups basmati rice, washed and drained
2 green chilies, seeded and sliced

Dry Masala:
2 teaspoons salt
1¹/₂ teaspoon ground nutmeg
1 rounded teaspoon sugar
1 teaspoon ground cinnamon
¹/₄ teaspoon ground clove

Pinch of saffron threads, soaked in 2 tablespoons of hot water for 10 minutes

3 cups chicken stock
1 cup fresh green peas
4 tablespoons raisins
2 tablespoons chopped coriander leaves for garnish

1. Make the marinade by putting the ingredients into a blender, first the lemon juice and the tomatoes, then the spices. Puree into a smooth paste. Combine the marinade with the oil and 1 cup of the yoghurt. Cover chicken pieces and let sit in refrigerator at least 4 hours and preferably overnight.

2. In a wok or heavy skillet, heat half the butter. Add half the onion rings and saute until translucent. Add the chicken pieces and brown on all sides, about 5 minutes. (Do half the pieces at a time if they do not all fit comfortably in the pan.) Stir to keep chicken from sticking. Reduce heat and pour the marinade over the meat. Cover and simmer until chicken is cooked, about 20 minutes. Uncover and *bhoona* to evaporate most of the liquid. Remove from stove and set aside.

3. Preheat oven to 350°F.

4. Wash and drain the rice. Meanwhile, in a large casserole with a tight-fitting lid, heat the remaining butter just to the smoking point. Add the rest of the onions and saute until they begin to turn brown. Add the green chilies and the dry masala and stir-fry for 3 minutes. Sprinkle in the rice and the saffron and its liquid. *Bhoona* over medium high heat until rice becomes translucent.

NOTE: The dish may be prepared to this point and finished later.

5. Add the chicken stock to the rice and bring to a boil. Top with the chicken pieces, cover, and place in the oven. Using a fork, very lightly fold in the peas, raisins and the remaining yoghurt, fluffing the mixture carefully so as not to break the rice grains. Garnish with coriander leaves and serve.

Palace Nawabi Biryani
SPECIAL PALACE BIRYANI

Without the meat, this recipe becomes the Special Palace Pulao.

SERVES 6-8.

1 pound ($^1/_2$ kg) lean lamb, trimmed of all fat and cut into $^1/_2$ inch ($1^1/_2$ cm) cubes

2 pounds (1 kg) basmati rice (no substitute)

8 ounces (250 gm) butter (2 sticks)

1 onion, chopped fine

Full Masala
8 peppercorns
6 whole cloves
2 cinnamon sticks 2 inches long (5 cm)

4 black cardamom pods, crushed

1 tablespoon garlic/ginger paste, or
3 garlic cloves, mashed
1 piece fresh ginger, size of walnut, minced

$^1/_2$ teaspoon salt
$^1/_2$ teaspoon paprika
$^1/_2$ teaspoon garam masala (optional)

2 cups water
$^1/_2$ cup milk

1. Prepare lamb and set aside. Pick over the rice and rinse in a colander until water runs clear. Set rice aside to soak in water to cover for at least 15 minutes.

2. In a wok or heavy skillet with a tight-fitting lid melt the butter over medium heat. Add the onion and the full masala and *bhoona* until onion turns golden. Add the garlic/ginger paste, salt, and paprika and garam masala. (For *bhoona* technique, see p. 13.)

3. Add the meat and *bhoona* for 10 minutes over medium heat, stirring constantly so that it does not scorch.

It may be necessary to add a few spoonfuls of water during the *bhoona-ing*. Finally, add 2 cups of water, cover and simmer for $^1/_2$ hour. Stir gently every 10 minutes so meat will not scorch.

4. Add the rice and the milk, plus enough water to cover the rice to a depth of 1 inch (3 cm). Bring to a boil, cover tightly, and simmer over lowest heat 15 minutes. Turn off heat and let the mixture sit—without lifting the lid—for another 5 minutes. Just before serving, lightly fluff the rice, using a fork so as not to break the rice grains.

NOTE: You may dribble some fresh lemon juice over the meat just before serving.

Tarkari Biryani
VEGETABLE BIRYANI

SERVES 6-8.

*¹/₂ cup carrots, cut in ¹/₂-inch
   (2 cm) cubes*
¹/₂ cup green beans, diced
¹/₂ cup cauliflower buds, diced
1 ounce (30 gm) raisins
*1 ounce (30 gm) sliced
   almonds*
*2 pound basmati rice (no
   substitute)*
*8 ounces (250 gm) butter (2
   sticks)*
1 onion, chopped fine

Full Masala:
8 peppercorns
6 whole cloves

*2 cinnamon sticks 2 inches (5
   cm) long*
*4 black cardamom pods,
   crushed*

*1 tablespoon garlic/ginger
   paste or*
   3 garlic cloves, mashed
   *1 piece fresh ginger, size of
      walnut, minced*
¹/₂ teaspoon salt
1 teaspoon paprika
1 teaspoon garam masala
¹/₂ cup milk
¹/₂ cup fresh green peas

1. Plunge the carrots, green beans and cauliflower into boiling water and blanch for 3 minutes. Drain, and set aside. Saute the raisins and almonds in a bit of butter until almonds turn golden. Set aside. Clean and wash rice in a colander under a faucet until the water runs clear. Set rice aside to soak in water to cover at least 15 minutes.

2. In a wok or heavy skillet with a tight-fitting lid, melt the butter over medium heat. Add the onions and the full masala and *bhoona* until onions turn golden. Stir in the garlic/ginger paste, salt, paprika and garam masala.

3. Drain rice and add it, plus the milk and enough water to cover the rice to a depth of 1 inch (3 cm). Bring to a boil, cover tightly, and simmer over lowest heat for 15 minutes. After 10 minutes, very gently stir in the blanched vegetables, the raisins and almonds, and the fresh peas. Re-cover and finish cooking the rice. When rice is done, turn off the heat and let rest for 5 minutes. Do not lift lid during this steaming period. Just before serving, fluff the rice, gently lifting from the bottom with a fork so as not to break the grains.

Gosht Biryani
LAMB OR BEEF BIRYANI

SERVES 2-4.

1 pound (¹/₂ kg) lamb or beef
  trimmed of all fat, boned
  and cut into 2-inch (5 cm)
  cubes
¹/₂ cup (120 gm) butter (1
  stick)
5 onions, chopped
1 garlic clove, minced
1 cup yoghurt

Dry Masala:
2 teaspoons ground coriander
1 teaspoon ground ginger
1 teaspoon ground cardamom

¹/₂ teaspoon red chili powder
¹/₄ teaspoon ground cinnamon
¹/₄ teaspoon ground cloves
a pinch of saffron soaked in 2
  tablespoons hot water for 10
  minutes

5 cups chicken or beef stock,
  warmed
1 cup long grain rice, basmati
  preferred
salt and freshly ground pepper
  to taste

1. Prepare lamb or beef and set aside.

2. In a wok or heavy skillet melt one-third of the butter. Add one-half of the onions and saute until translucent. Add garlic and saute 1 minute. Remove onion and garlic mixture and set aside.

3. Add the meat to the pot and brown on all sides over medium heat. Return the onions to the pot, and add the yoghurt and the dry masala. Add 2 cups of stock (enough to cover the meat) and simmer, covered, until tender, about 30 minutes.

4. In a small pot heat another third of butter and saute the remaining onions until softened. Add the rice and continue sauteing, stirring constantly, until rice is translucent, about 3 minutes. Add the saffron and its liquid and enough stock to cover the rice, bring to boil, cover, and turn heat to lowest flame. Let steam, undisturbed, for 15 minutes. Meanwhile, preheat the oven to 350°F.

5. In an ovenproof serving dish alternate the rice and the lamb in layers. Put remaining butter on top, cover the dish and set it in the oven for 5 minutes before serving.

Chapter 12

BREADS
(Roti)

While many think of India as a rice-consuming nation, no other country in the world makes such a delicious variety of breads. While some of these treats are made from lentil or rice flour, many are made from wheat, an inheritance from the wheat-eating Moghuls of the North.

There are many kinds of Indian breads, most of them quite easy to prepare and all of them delicious. There are many regional variations, but the most popular breads are chapatis (in a smaller form called *kulchas*), parathas and pooris. Nan is a bread made especially to be cooked in a tandoor oven. The teardrop-shaped dough is slapped onto the inside of the fiery hot clay oven, baked in about 3 minutes, then pulled off with an iron hook. This fast baking leaves the outside of the nan bubbly and brown-flaked, an appetizing appearance that cannot be obtained when baking the nan in an ordinary oven. However we have a successful substitute method to offer here.

Most Indian breads contain no yeast and so are easier to prepare than Western bread. Since they do not rise but cook flat, they also bake faster than Western types. Indian breads are also quite healthful since they contain no sugar or eggs and only the richer breads have just a little butter.

There are two things of importance in making Indian breads successfully: the proper flour mixture, and correct kneading.

PROPER FLOUR MIXTURE

While many different grain mixtures are used in India, a very satisfactory all-purpose substitute to use is roughly 3 parts of all-purpose unbleached white flour to 1 part whole wheat flour.

This mixture makes a "lighter" dough and also helps to turn the cooked bread a golden color. You can also buy ready-mixed chapati flour in Indian specialty shops in the United States.

TO KNEAD THE DOUGH

The optimum amount of water to use may vary with humidity and temperature, so the amounts given in the recipes are only approximate. However, it is important not to use any more water than necessary to turn out a soft dough, very much like a pizza dough. Knead it for 10 to 15 minutes, and then let it rest for at least half an hour (an hour is even better), before shaping. This resting of the dough is quite important because it relaxes the dough and makes it easier to roll out. The simplest way to rest the dough without letting it dry out is to place it in a very lightly greased bowl, cover the bowl with a sheet of plastic, and set the bowl in a warm place, such as the inside of an oven warmed only by its pilot light.

No special equipment is needed to bake good Indian breads. In India a slightly concave iron griddle called the *tava* is used, but a 9-inch heavy-bottomed cast iron skillet will do just fine. One final tip: In rolling out the circles of dough, give the rolling pin a slight twist toward the edge of the dough and you will make perfect circles. And, of course, each circle must be of the same thickness as all the others.

Keep the baked breads warm in a bowl covered by a napkin until ready to serve. Breads may be reheated by sprinkling just a few drops of water on them, enclosing them in a foil wrapper, and placing in a 350°F oven for about 15 minutes.

Indian breads are also a fine accompaniment to almost any Western-style meal.

Chapatis or Roti

Chapatis (roti is merely the Punjabi word for them) are delicious flat cakes similar to parathas except that they are thinner and they are not buttered.

MAKES ABOUT 20 PIECES.

1¹/₂ cups (175 gm) unbleached
  white flour
¹/₂ cup (60 gm) whole wheat
  flour

1 rounded teaspoon salt
3 tablespoons (45 gm) oil or
  butter
¹/₂ to ³/₄ cup water

1. Mix the first four ingredients and add just enough water to make a firm dough, somewhat like a biscuit dough. Knead for 10-15 minutes—the more the dough is kneaded the lighter the bread will be. Shape the dough into a ball, cover with a sheet of plastic and let it rest for at least 1 hour. If left to rest overnight in the refrigerator the finished bread will be even lighter.

2. When ready to bake, take a small piece of dough about the size of a golf ball, or a bit smaller. On a lightly floured board, roll the dough into a thin circle, about 5 inches (13 cm) in diameter. Repeat with all the dough.

3. Heat a griddle or heavy-bottomed iron skillet until it is very hot (you will notice the smoke rising from it). Place the rolled-out chapati on the griddle *(tava)* and let it cook for 2-3 minutes, depending on how thin you have rolled it. Using a pair of kitchen tongs, you can lift the chapati to see if the underside has turned a golden brown. Flip, and cook the other side about 1 minute.

As they are cooked, store the chapatis on a towel in a warm covered container until ready to serve. Serve as soon as the last chapati is baked.

NOTE: In India breads sometimes are baked in the fiery clay tandoor, where they develop brown spots and bubbles. To achieve a similar effect at home, you can use tongs to hold each chapati directly over a hot gas flame until it puffs like a little balloon. The chapati will collapse as it cools.

Nan

1¹/₂ cups (175 gm) unbleached
white flour
¹/₂ cup (60 gm) whole wheat
flour
4 eggs
1 cup heavy cream

1 teaspoon salt
1¹/₂ teaspoon baking powder
¹/₄ teaspoon baking soda
Small bowl of oil or melted
butter for greasing the nan,
plus 2 ounces (60 ml)

1. Mix all ingredients except the oil to make a soft dough (like pizza), and knead 10-15 minutes. Add 2 ounces (60 ml) of oil or melted butter and knead again for 5-8 minutes. Form into a ball, cover with a damp cloth and let rise in a warm place until double in size. When the dough is ready, a finger pressed into the dough will leave an impression. This will take from 1 to 2 hours depending on temperature and humidity.

2. Divide dough into 8-10 balls. Dipping your fingers into the bowl of oil or butter, lightly pat each ball to coat with fat. Cover again with damp cloth and let rest for 15 minutes.

3. Meanwhile preheat oven to 450°F.

4. Wet your palms with oil or butter and pat each ball into a flat circle, making the circle thinner in the center and a tiny bit thicker at the edge. Pull one side to make the circle into a teardrop shape. Each nan should be about the size of your hand.

5. Place the nan on a cooky sheet and brush the tops with oil or butter. Bake 10-12 minutes until the nan become puffy. To make them a perfect golden color, place the baked nan under a broiler for a minute or two. Serve at once.

Paratha, Home-Style

MAKES 10-12 PIECES.

1¹/₂ cups (175 gm) all-purpose
   unbleached white flour
1¹/₂ cups (60 gm) whole wheat
   flour
¹/₂ teaspoon salt

4 ounces (120 gm) butter (1
   stick)
1 to 1¹/₂ cups water
3 ounces (90 ml) melted butter
   to grease the paratha

1. Mix the two flours and salt in a large bowl.

2. Melt the butter in 2 tablespoons of water and add to the flour. Form into a ball of dough and transfer the ball to a flat, lightly floured surface.

3. Knead for 10-15 minutes, until the dough becomes firm but not stiff (like a pizza dough). The more kneading the lighter the dough. Shape dough into a ball, cover with a plastic sheet, and let rest for ¹/₂ hour to 1 hour in a warm place, such as an oven with a pilot light.

4. Lightly flour a smooth surface and roll the dough out into a circle about 18 inches (45 cm) in diameter and ³/₄ inch (2 cm) thick. Brush with melted butter and roll up like a jelly roll. Slice into 10-12 pieces about ³/₄ inches (2 cm) thick.

5. Take one piece and cover the rest with a damp cloth. Roll the dough out into a thin circle. If the circle breaks, pinch off a bit of dough from the edge to patch it. Lightly butter the circle. With a sharp knife, make a cut from its center to one edge. Now roll the dough into a cone, tuck in the bottom end and push down with the flat of the hand until you once again have a small circle. Dust with flour and, using light pressure, roll out into a flat circle about ¹/₈ inch thick and about 8 inches in diameter (¹/₂ cm × 20 cm).

6. Repeat with the rest of the dough. When all the parathas have been formed, lightly butter and heat a heavy-bottomed 9-inch (23 cm) skillet over medium-high heat. Add a paratha and cook for 2 or 3 minutes, until the under side begins to turn spotted brown. Lightly butter top side, flip over and cook the second side about 1 minute. Butter the new top side and flip over after 1 minute. The finished paratha should be a dusky golden color, prettily spotted with brown flecks.

7. The parathas should be covered and kept warm until the batch is finished. Serve as quickly as possible.

NOTE: Leftover parathas can be reheated the next day by wrapping in foil and heating 15 minutes in a 350°F oven.

Pooris

These are delightful "balloon" breads that are not only intriguing to look at but wonderfully tasty. These are basically the same as a chapati but instead of being cooked on a griddle they are puffed in hot oil.

NOTE: Since these airy puffs are perishable, wait to cook them until just before you are ready to serve the meal. Allow about ½ hours in all for rolling out and frying.

If you do not care about serving them in their puffed state, poori can be kept for half an hour by wrapping them in aluminum foil and keeping them in a warm, covered container. They can even be reheated by being foil-wrapped and set in a 350°F oven for 15 minutes.

MAKES ABOUT 10 PIECES.

1. Prepare dough for making poori as for chapatis (p. 163). Roll out the dough into thin 5-inch (12 cm) circles, and store them in a moist cloth.

2. When ready to fry, cover the bottom of a wok or heavy skillet with about 2 inches (5 cm) of oil and heat it to 400°F. At this temperature a faint haze will rise from the surface.

3. Drop in one poori at a time and immediately begin spooning hot oil over it to make it puff. When the poori begins to puff, pat it very gently with the bottom of a spoon for about 3 seconds. This will increase the puffing. When the poori stops sizzling and the under side is lightly brown (a few seconds to half a minute), flip it and set it on a paper towel to drain. Proceed with the rest of the batch, as swiftly as possible.

4. The poori will stay puffed for only about 5 minutes, so they must be served at once.

Luchi

This crisp and puffy bread is a tasty specialty from Bengal. The procedure is almost identical to making poori, except the dough is made with 2 tablespoons additional butter and the luchi are rolled out as thin as possible, even thinner than chapati.

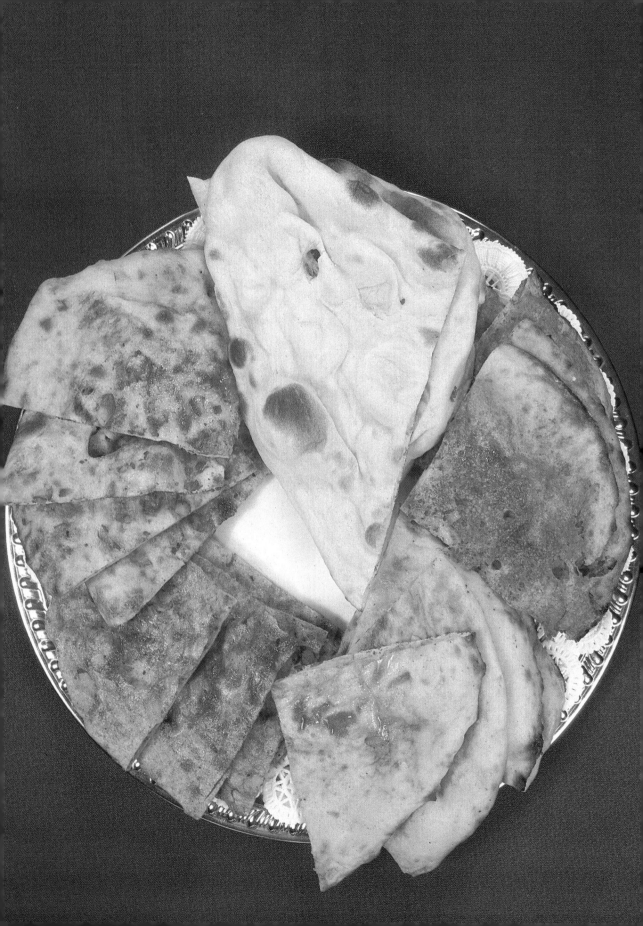

Stuffed Indian Breads

Indian breads are even more delicious when they are stuffed with various fillings. They also make a good accompaniment for cocktails. Here are some variations as prepared in the Bombay Palace. You can also use your imagination to make up your own combinations of vegetables and spices.

Murgh Masala Nan
NAN STUFFED WITH CHICKEN AND SPICES

MAKES 8-10 PIECES.

Filling:
*1 cup cooked boneless
chicken, minced*

1 large onion, minced
2 tablespoons (30 gm) butter

1. Prepare the dough and shape the nan according to instructions (p. 164).

2. To prepare filling, saute the minced onion in the butter until golden and blend well with the cooked chicken.

3. Put 2 tablespoons of the filling in the center of each nan. Fold over and very gently roll out to reshape the nan. Pull one edge gently to form a teardrop shape. Be careful not to break the dough.

4. Bake the nan in the regular manner. Serve hot.

Onion Kulcha
NAN STUFFED WITH ONIONS AND SPICES

MAKES 8-10 PIECES.

2 onions, minced
$1/4$ teaspoon salt
generous grinding of black
  pepper
2 tablespoons chopped
  coriander leaves, loosely
  packed

OPTIONAL: Add either one
  or both, according to taste:
1 teaspoon red chili powder
$1/2$ teaspoon dried mango
  powder (amchoor)

1. Prepare nan recipe through step 4.

2. Prepare onions; add salt, coriander leaves and optional seasonings.

3. After rolling out and shaping each nan, put 2 teaspoons of the onion mixture in the center of each piece of dough. Pinch the dough together to cover the spices, then turn it over and very gently roll it out again to a circle about the size of your hand, being careful not to break the dough. Pull one edge gently to form a teardrop shape.

4. Bake the nan in the regular manner. Serve hot.

Keema Paratha
PARATHA STUFFED WITH MINCED MEAT

MAKES 10-12 PIECES.

Filling:
$1/2$ pound boneless meat
  (chicken, lamb, beef, etc.),
  minced

$1/2$ onion, minced fine
$1/4$ teaspoon salt
generous grinding of black
  pepper

1. Mix together the chopped meat, onion, salt and pepper and cook in wok or heavy skillet with no additional fat just until the meat loses its pinkness.

2. Make the paratha dough (p. 165), and roll out as for regular parathas.

3. Put 2 tablespoons of the meat mixture in the center of each paratha. Carefully fold over to cover the mixture, and very gently roll out into circles about 8 inches (20 cm) in diameter, being careful not to break the dough. Bake in the regular manner. Serve hot.

Moghlai Paratha
LAMB-FILLED PARATHA

Filling:
*1/2 pound raw lean lamb,
chopped fine*
1 onion, minced
1/4 teaspoon salt

*generous grinding of black
pepper*
4 eggs
*1 teaspoon chopped coriander
leaves*

1. Mix the filling ingredients well. Set aside.

2. Make the paratha dough and roll out in circles about 12 inches (30 cm) in diameter. Put 3 tablespoons of the filling in the center of each circle and fold four times to make a square pocket, leaving a small opening about 1/2 inch (1 1/2 cm) in the center, to allow steam to escape during baking. Fry the stuffed parathas in the regular manner, turning with special care to avoid breaking.

3. As soon as the Moghlai parathas are baked, cut each one twice diagonally with a sharp knife, to make four triangular pieces. Stack the parathas on a warm plate, overlapping the base of each triangle with the apex of the next, so they form a sort of Christmas-tree pattern. Serve while hot.

Aloo Paratha
POTATO-FILLED PARATHAS

MAKES 10-12 PIECES.

1 recipe parathas

Filling:
3 tablespoons (45 gm) butter
1 onion, minced
2 garlic cloves, minced
1 piece fresh ginger, size of
   walnut, minced
2 large potatoes, peeled, boiled
   and mashed, or:
   1 1/2 cups cooked chopped
   cabbage

2 green chilies, seeded and
   minced
1 teaspoon salt
generous grinding of black
   pepper
1 1/2 teaspoons chopped
   coriander leaves
1 teaspoon ground cumin
1 teaspoon garam masala (p.
   15-19)

1. In a wok or heavy skillet, heat the butter. Add the onions, garlic and ginger and saute until onion becomes translucent. Add the rest of the ingredients and stir-fry until moisture evaporates, about 6 minutes.

2. Make paratha dough and roll out in circles about 8 inches (20 cm) in diameter. Put 2 tablespoons of the filling in the center of each circle, fold over to cover the filling, and very gently roll out again into 8 inch (20 cm) circles. Fry in the regular paratha manner. Serve hot.

Gobhi Parathas
CAULIFLOWER-FILLED PARATHAS

MAKES 10-12 PIECES.

1 recipe parathas

Filling:
2 tablespoons (30 gm) butter
1 cup of tender cauliflower
   buds, chopped fine
1 piece fresh ginger, size of
   Brazil nut, minced

1 teaspoon salt
freshly ground black pepper
1 rounded teaspoon garam
   masala
1 teaspoon red chili powder

1. In a wok or heavy skillet melt the butter and stir-fry the cauliflower until it loses its moisture and starts to soften.

2. Add remainder of ingredients and mix well, stirring for 2 minutes. Remove from heat and cool.

3. Make paratha dough and roll out in circles about 8 inches (20 cm) in diameter. Put 2 tablespoons of the filling in the center of each circle, fold over to cover the filling and very gently roll out again into 8-inch (20 cm) circles. Fry the Gobi Parathas in the regular manner. Serve hot.

Chapter 13

LENTILS
AND LEGUMES

Legumes are the edible seeds of the widely distributed plant family that includes peas, beans, lentils and chick-peas. These highly nutritious vegetables are extremely popular all over India, either as side dishes or the ever present dals, which are basically spiced lentils, either pureed or served whole. Whether served with rice or one of the tasty Indian breads, this delicious concoction is present at every Indian meal.

TYPES OF LEGUMES

Legumes or pulse fall into three broad categories: beans, lentils and peas. The types most used in the Indian cuisine are:

BEANS   Black gram bean, mung beans, pink beans, red kidney beans

LENTILS   Pink or salmon lentils, yellow lentils, black lentils

PEAS   Yellow split peas, whole chick-peas (garbanzos or ceci), black-eyed peas

Here is a list of the commonly used dals:

ARHAR or TOOVAR DAL   Yellow split peas.

CHANA DAL Chick-peas, hulled and split. These should not be confused with the common supermarket variety, a different species that does not turn golden yellow when cooked.

CHOTI RAJMA Pink beans

KALA CHANA Small black chick-peas, whole or unhulled

LOBHIA Whole black-eyed peas

MASOOR DAL Pink or salmon lentils, hulled and split. These turn yellow when cooked.

MOOG DAL Mung beans; small and green when whole, yellow when hulled and split

RAJMA or BADI RAJMA Red kidney beans

URAD DAL Black gram bean; hulled and split, they are ivory in color

In the less expensive Indian restaurants in the West, too often dal is overly thin. A pureed dal is not a soup; its consistency should be thinner than cooked cereal but thicker than a pea soup. Each Indian state has its own style of preparing legumes and pulse, and the variations are endless. We present just a few of the more popular dal and lentil dishes here.

CLEANING AND WASHING:

All legumes and pulse should be picked over carefully before washing. Spread a handful of the beans or lentils on a large plate and sift through them, discarding any small stones or other foreign matter. Then put the lentils in a fine-mesh sieve and wash under cold running water, shaking the sieve to clean well. Soaking procedures, where needed, are described for each recipe.

NOTE: It is best to discard all soaking liquid and start with fresh water for cooking. Also discard any legumes that are floating on top of the soak water.

Moog Dal
SPLIT MUNG BEAN DAL

SERVES 8.

1 cup split mung beans
6 cups water

Dry Masala:
1 teaspoon ground coriander
1 teaspoon red pepper flakes
$^1/_2$ teaspoon turmeric

1 bay leaf
6 cardamom seeds, crushed
salt to taste
2 tablespoons (30 gm) butter
  ($^1/_4$ stick)
2 onions, chopped
sprinkle of paprika for garnish

1. Pick over lentils carefully to remove grit or stones. Put in saucepan, along with the dry masala, the bay leaf and the cardamom seeds. Cover with 6 cups water and simmer for $^1/_2$ hour.

2. Remove from heat and puree the lentils in a blender until the mixture is thick and smooth. Add salt to taste.

3. In a wok or heavy skillet heat the butter and saute the onions until golden brown. Stir into the dal, sprinkle the top with paprika and serve.

Mung Ki Dal
MUNG BEAN DAL

SERVES 4.

1 cup hulled mung beans
1 teaspoon turmeric
1 teaspoon salt
2 green chilies, seeded and
   sliced lengthwise
4 tablespoons (60 gm) butter
   (1/2 stick)

1 teaspoon mustard seeds
1 onion, thinly sliced and
   separated into rings
1 garlic clove, minced
1/2 teaspoon red chili flakes

1. Pick over the mung beans and wash in cold running water until the water runs clear. Soak the beans for 4 hours.

2. Drain the beans and put into a wok or saucepan. Add the turmeric, salt and green chilies. Cover this mixture with 1 inch of water and bring to a boil. Partly cover, reduce heat and simmer for 1 hour, or until water is absorbed and the dal is tender but not mushy. Add a bit more hot water during cooking if necessary.

3. Meanwhile in a wok or heavy skillet heat the butter, add the mustard seeds and stir-fry for 2 minutes. When the seeds start to hop, carefully remove the pan from the heat and add the onion rings and garlic. Replace on stove and stir-fry until onions are golden. Stir in the red chili flakes. Mix well then add the dal. Stir over high heat for 2 minutes to blend.

175

Kitchuri
LENTILS WITH RICE

Kitcheri, a mixture of lentils and rice, is an authentic Indian dish. It is sometimes confused with Kedgeree, a boiled rice and fish concoction that evolved to suit the taste of British colonials stationed in India. The proportions of rice to lentils may be varied from equal quantities to 3 parts rice to 1 part lentils, depending on preference.

SERVES 4.

1 ½ cups basmati rice
1 ½ cups orange lentils
   (masoor dal)
½ cup (120 gm) butter (1
   stick)
2 onions, chopped fine
1 tablespoon garlic/ginger
   paste or
   3 garlic cloves, mashed
   1 piece fresh ginger, size of
      walnut, minced

1 teaspoon salt
1 teaspoon turmeric
2 tablespoons coconut milk (p.
   35) or use regular milk
boiling water

Garnish:
1 large onion, thinly sliced
1 tablespoon (15 gm) butter

1. Wash rice and lentils together in cold running water until water runs clear.

2. In a wok or large saucepan melt the butter and add the onions and the garlic/ginger paste and stir-fry until onions are golden.

3. Drain the rice and lentils well and add them to the pan, stirring constantly for 2 minutes. Add the salt and turmeric and stir-fry 5 minutes.

4. Pour in sufficient boiling water to cover by ½ inch. When the water bubbles and wells begin to appear in the mixture, cover and simmer for 20 minutes.

5. Meanwhile prepare the garnish. Fry the onion rings in butter until crisp and golden. Drain on absorbent paper and keep warm.

6. Remove rice/lentil mixture from heat and let sit, covered, for 5 minutes. Fluff gently with fork and transfer to a heated serving dish. Drizzle coconut milk or regular milk on top, garnish with fried onions and serve.

Dal Maharani
MIXED CREAMED DAL

This recipe calls for asafetida, for which onion may be substituted. It also calls for the spiced "butter" known as tardka.

SERVES 4-6.

1 cup black lentils (kala
   chana)
8 cups water
1/2 cup kidney beans (rajma)
1/2 cup small split chick-peas
   (chana dal)

Dry Masala:
1/2 teaspoon ground turmeric
1/4 teaspoon red pepper flakes
salt and freshly ground pepper
   to taste

4 teaspoons mustard oil
1/4 teaspoon asafetida, or
   substitute 1/2 small onion,
   minced
1 piece fresh ginger, size of
   walnut, minced
1/2 cup tardka
2 tablespoons chopped
   coriander leaves for garnish

1. Clean and wash the lentils. Let soak 2 hours. Put into a pot with 8 cups of water and bring to a boil.

2. Add the dry masala, the asafetida or onion, the ginger and mustard oil. Partly cover and simmer until lentils open and are tender—about 1 to 1 1/2 hours. If necessary, add enough hot water to keep the lentils covered during cooking. Set aside.

3. When ready to serve, add 1/2 cup tardka to the lentils. Warm over low heat, mixing well.

4. Garnish with chopped coriander before serving.

Chana Pindi
CHICK-PEAS, PINDI STYLE

Pindi is a town in the Punjab. This recipe calls for chana masala, one of many mixed condiment packages obtainable at an Indian food shop. If you have none, substitute a rounded tablespoon of my full-flavored garam masala (p. 22) for each half-packet of the chana masala. In Indian markets whole chick-peas are called gram dal.

SERVES 4-6.

1/2 pound chick-peas (gram dal), about 1 cup (225 gm)

Dry Masala:
1/2 packet chana masala or:
1 rounded tablespoon garam masala (see note above)
1/2 teaspoon ground coriander
1/2 teaspoon ground cumin
1/2 teaspoon paprika
1/2 teaspoon turmeric
1/4 teaspoon red chili powder

2 tomatoes, coarsely chopped

1 piece fresh ginger, size of Brazil nut, minced
1/2 cup water
2 ounces (60 gm) butter (1/2 stick)
salt and freshly ground pepper to taste

Garnish:
1/2 packet chana masala or:
1 rounded tablespoon garam masala (see note above)
2 tablespoons chopped coriander leaves
1 teaspoon garam masala

1. Clean, then soak the chick-peas in water for at least 2 hours. Bring chick-peas to boil in water to cover, with a bit of salt added. Boil for 3 minutes, removing any scum that may form. Cover and simmer until tender, about 40 minutes, adding more hot water if needed. Drain, put in a bowl and set aside.

2. Blend the dry masala and stir into the chick-peas. Stir in the ginger and the tomatoes.

3. To a wok or heavy skillet, add the chick-pea mixture plus 1/2 cup of water, cover, and simmer until liquid evaporates, 5 to 7 minutes. Put the chick-peas into a serving bowl.

4. In a separate pan melt the butter. Pour this over the chick-peas. Add the second 1/2 packet of chana masala, sprinkle with coriander leaves, and finally sprinkle with garam masala.

This dish is good either hot or at room temperature.

Chapter 14

ACCOMPANIMENTS

Chutneys are something like our Western preserves, only served in many more varieties. They range in taste from sweet to spicy to sour to blistering hot. Pickles are similar to chutneys except that they are usually both intensely salty and fiery in taste.

Sweet mango chutney (the familiar Major Grey type) makes a soothing counterpoint to spicy dishes, and is certainly the most well-known chutney in the West. It is probably of British colonial origin, hence the name.

In India, chutneys are made fresh daily, but you can make up a batch of chutney ahead of time and store it in the refrigerator to be used several days in a row.

In addition to pickles and chutneys, raita, a yoghurt-based concoction, is a popular accompaniment and provides a soothing counterpoint to the spicy main dishes so characteristic of Indian cookery.

Seb Chatni
APPLE CHUTNEY

SERVES 3 or 4.

1 large tart apple, peeled and
minced
1 large green pepper, seeded
and minced

3/4 teaspoon paprika
1/2 teaspoon red pepper flakes
1 1/2 teaspoons lemon juice
1/4 teaspoon salt

Core the apple before mincing. Scald the pepper before seeding. Mince both very fine and mix them thoroughly. Add the paprika and pepper flakes and mix thoroughly. Add lemon juice and salt, and mix well again.

Hara Dhania Chatni
FRESH CORIANDER-COCONUT CHUTNEY

MAKES ABOUT 1 CUP.

2/3 cup yoghurt
2 heaping tablespoons fresh
shredded coconut
(unsweetened)
1 bunch coriander leaves, plus
half the stalks

2 green chilies, seeded
1 teaspoon salt
1 teaspoon sugar
juice of half a lemon

Mix the coconut and the yoghurt and set aside for 1 hour. Place all ingredients in a blender and puree. Add more lemon juice if needed to make puree smooth. Adjust seasoning. Chill.

Dhania Poodina
CORIANDER-MINT SAUCE

MAKES 1 CUP.

1/3 cup yoghurt
3/4 cup packed fresh coriander
 leaves
1/4 cup packed fresh mint
 leaves
1/4 green pepper, seeded and
 chopped

2 green chilies, seeded
1 tablespoon chopped onion
1 piece fresh ginger, size of
 almond
3/4 teaspoon sugar
2 tablespoons water

Put all ingredients in a food processor or blender and puree until smooth. Cover and chill before serving.

Dhania Mirch Chatni
CORIANDER-CHILI CHUTNEY

MAKES ABOUT 2 CUPS.

1 cup loosely packed fresh
 coriander leaves
1 fresh green chili
3 tablespoons cold water
1/2 teaspoon cumin seeds

1 cup yoghurt
1 tablespoon lemon juice
1/4 teaspoon salt
light grinding white pepper
 (optional)

1. In a blender or food processor put the coriander leaves and the green chili. Add 3 tablespoons of water and puree to a smooth paste. Turn off blender and scrape down mixture with rubber spatula if necessary. Scrape the mixture into a bowl.

2. Put the cumin seeds in a small fry pan and roast them over low heat until they start to dance. Put in a mortar and crush to coarse powder.

3. Add cumin powder, yoghurt, lemon juice, salt and pepper (optional) to coriander mixture. Stir to blend thoroughly and chill before serving.

Raita
SPICED YOGHURT WITH CUCUMBER

SERVES 4-6.

Cool and refreshing, raitas are served along with chutneys as a contrast to rich and pungent dishes.

RAITA # 1

*1 cucumber, peeled and minced
  (or grated)
2 cups yoghurt (1 pound; 1/2 kg)
1 cup yoghurt
1 teaspoon sugar
1/2 teaspoon salt*

*generous grinding of pepper
  (white pepper may be used
  for an all-white appearance)*

*1/4 teaspoon ground coriander
1/4 teaspoon ground cumin*

coriander leaves for garnish

Mix all ingredients well. Serve in a ceramic bowl ringed with fresh coriander leaves.

RAITA # 2

Follow previous recipe with these variations: If desired, the cucumber can be sliced into very thin rounds. For the ground cumin, substitute 1/2 teaspoon toasted cumin seeds. *To toast cumin seeds:* Place the seeds in a small skillet. Over low heat toast and shake the seeds until they begin to turn dark and give off a fragrant, nutty aroma. Mix and serve as before.

Katchumber Salad
CUCUMBER SALAD

SERVES 4.

2 cucumbers, peeled and cut
   into small dice
2 onions, chopped fine
2 tomatoes, in small dice
2 teaspoons oil

juice of 1/2 lemon
1/4 teaspoon salt and grinding
   of fresh pepper
4 lettuce leaves for garnish

Mix all ingredients and set on a lettuce leaf on each place. Serve cold.

Piaz Aur Tamatar Sambal
ONION AND TOMATO SAMBAL

Sambals are relishes commonly used in South India. They are sometimes served hot, but more often cold, along with raitas and chutneys.

MAKES ABOUT 11/2 CUPS.

2 tomatoes, chopped fine
1 onion, chopped fine
1 green chili, seeded and
   chopped fine
1 tablespoon coriander leaves,
   chopped
1/2 teaspoon salt

1/2 teaspoon sugar
2 tablespoons lemon juice
generous grinding of pepper,
   preferably white
1 tablespoon freshly grated
   coconut

Combine all ingredients except the coconut in a shallow serving bowl. Sprinkle coconut on top. Chill thoroughly before serving.

Bhoone Piaz Ke Kache
CRISPY CARAMELIZED ONIONS

Many of our recipes call for crispy caramelized onion rings as a garnish, and they are essential to any do piaza recipe. Onion rings are also delicious just for nibbling, by themselves or with a cocktail. If you make them ahead of time, be sure to seal them in an airtight container or they will become soggy. Use them the same day you make them, in any case.

Crispy onions are one of the unique contributions the Indians have made to world cooking. The concept is to slow-cook the onions until they become very dark and caramelized without turning black or scorching. This takes a good deal longer than we ordinarily think of cooking onions, but the sweet dark taste and crunchy texture makes the effort worthwhile. The onions are either gently folded into a dish or sprinkled on top. Either way, their unusual taste and texture should be separate from the other ingredients in the dish. Crispy onions, when crumbled, make an interesting color addition to a pilaf or biryani.

MAKES ABOUT 2 CUPS.

3 large onions
3 tablespoons oil

Peel the onions and very carefully slice as thin as possible. Gently separate into rings with your fingers. Heat the oil in a wok or heavy skillet over a medium flame until hot but not smoking. Add the onion rings and stir constantly until they become a glossy brown. Continue cooking until onions become crisp, at least 20 minutes. Drain them on paper towels and use them immediately or seal in an airtight container.

Chapter 15

DESSERTS
AND DRINKS

In the West, most Indian restaurants offer a very limited range of desserts. On the Indian continent, however, a wide variety of puddings and other sweets are devoured by natives throughout the day. At festivals and markets, sweets vendors make little cakes and candies that are gobbled up by young and old alike.

Ice cream, or kulfi, is the all-time favorite dessert, in India as in the West.

Kulfi
INDIAN "ICE CREAM"

SERVES 6-8.

1 13-ounce can (¹/₃ liter)
   sweetened condensed milk
1 cup heavy cream

¹/₄ cup each almond and
   pistachio nuts, chopped fine
¹/₂ teaspoon vanilla

1. Prepare nuts, which may be chopped easily in a blender. Mix all ingredients together.

2. Pour into an ice cube tray and freeze until solid. Serve each person 2 cubes of kulfi.

NOTE: The dessert must be served as soon as it is taken from the ice tray, since it melts very quickly.

Kulfi
INDIAN "ICE CREAM" WITH PISTACHIO

While it is less time-consuming to prepare kulfi with sweet-ened condensed milk, this recipe is traditional and authentic.

SERVES 6.

2 quarts (2 liters) milk
1 pint (¹/₂ liter) heavy cream
12 ounces (340 gm) sugar

2 ounces (60 gm) pistachio
    nuts, ground

1. Pour the milk and the heavy cream into a wok or heavy bottomed skillet and bring to a boil. Boil gently for 40 minutes, stirring almost constantly with a wooden spoon, until the liquid is reduced by half.

2. Add the sugar and boil and stir constantly for another 15 minutes.

3. Pour into a freezer tray and chill in the freezer for at least 4 hours.

4. Before serving, sprinkle with the ground pistachios.

NOTE: This ice cream tastes better if it is made a day prior to use. Stored in the freezer the kulfi will last for about a month.

Sharbatee Gulab
ROSE PETAL-PINEAPPLE SHERBET

SERVES 6-8.

5 large roses
2 quarts (2 liters) cool (not
    iced) water
juice of 3 lemons

1¹/₃ cups sugar
3 cups pineapple, crushed
2 cups finely cracked ice

1. Wash roses thoroughly in cold wa-ter. Pick off all the petals, reserving a few for garnish; put the remainder in a large ceramic jar. Pour the cool wa-ter over them and set them aside in a dark place (away from any sunshine) for at least 4 hours.

2. Strain the rose water and discard petals.

3. Add the lemon juice and sugar to the rose water and stir until all sugar is dissolved. Add the pineapple and the cracked ice. Pour into glasses, top-ping each with a large fresh rose petal.

186

Gulab Jamun
ROSE-FLAVORED BALLS IN SUGAR SYRUP

These delicious little balls are painstaking to make but worth the effort. Great attention must be paid during the deep frying; the balls must be turned continually so that they take on an even golden color on all sides.

MAKES 25-30 BALLS.

The Sugar Syrup:
2 pounds (1 kg) sugar
2 quarts plus 1 pint (2¹/₂ liters) water
2 tablespoons rose water (see facing page)

The Dough:
3 cups dry milk
1 cup flour
3 tablespoons baking powder
2¹/₂ cups heavy cream
3 pints (1¹/₂ liters) of oil for deep frying

1. Make the sugar syrup first: In a heavy saucepan bring the sugar and water to a boil, then let it thicken by cooking over medium heat for about 20 minutes. Add the rose water and keep the syrup warm at a low simmer.

2. In a large bowl mix the ingredients for the dough thoroughly to make a stiff batter. Let mixture sit for 10-15 minutes to set. Take a pinch of dough a little smaller than a golf ball and roll it between your palms to round it into a neat ball.

Repeat with the rest of the dough.

3. In a wok or heavy skillet, heat the oil over high heat until a haze begins to form, just before it begins to smoke. Carefully add the balls until the surface is covered. (If necessary cook the balls in more than one batch.) With a large spoon, start turning the balls just as they begin to take on color. After about 3 minutes, turn the heat down to medium-low, and continue to turn the balls until they acquire a rich mahogany color.

4. When the sweetmeats have achieved a luscious, deep color, turn the heat up to high for 2-3 minutes to add still more color and to firm the crust. Drain onto paper towels.

5. When drained, put the balls into a large bowl and pour the sugar syrup over them. Let them rest until the syrup reaches room temperature. They can now be eaten—but they will taste even better if allowed to "tighten" until the next day.

NOTE: Gulab Jamun will keep a week or more, stored in the refrigerator.

Rasomalai
DESSERT DUMPLINGS WITH WHIPPED CREAM AND PISTACHIOS

SERVES 10-12.

The Cheese:
2 quarts (2 liters) milk
1 cup heavy cream
1 cup white vinegar
1 teaspoon sugar
1 teaspoon flour

The Syrup:
2 quarts (2 liters) water
1 pound (¹/₂ kg) sugar

The Topping:
¹/₂ pint (120 ml) heavy cream
2 teaspoons sugar
1 teaspoon rose water,
 optional
2 tablespoons unsalted
 pistachios, slivered

1. Bring the milk and the cup of heavy cream just to the boil. Add the cup of vinegar and stir well. As soon as the mixture curdles, put the curds in a fine-mesh sieve and gently wash with warm water to rid the cheese of excess vinegar.

2. Wrap the cheese in a cheesecloth and squeeze out excess liquid. Set the bag of cheese in a colander and rest a heavy weight on it (up to 10 pounds [4 kg]). Let stand until the cheese is firm, about ¹/₂ hour. To the cheese add the teaspoon of sugar and the teaspoon of flour. Knead until very soft; this will take 2-3 minutes.

3. Pick up small bits of the doughy cheese and roll them between your palms until they become small circles, about 2 inches wide by ¹/₄-inch thick (5 cm x ¹/₂ cm).

4. Set 2 quarts of water to boiling (2 liters), adding the pound (¹/₂ kg) of sugar to make a syrup. Add the cheese disks, cover, and allow to come to a second boil. Lower the flame and cook, covered, for 20 minutes. Stir gently several times to separate the disks as they cook. Drain and let disks cool to room temperature. They are now ready for serving, or they can be kept refrigerated for up to a week.

TO SERVE: Make topping by whipping the heavy cream and stirring in the sugar, and the rose water, if used. Put two of the cheese disks on each plate and cover with the topping. Sprinkle with a few slivers of pistachio.

188

Aam Malai
MANGO ICE CREAM

Buy your mango, if you can, from an Indian or Caribbean shop. In any case, be sure to purchase a nice ripe one; an unripe mango will be too tart for this recipe. Out of season, you can find mango pulp in cans.

SERVES 6-8.

1 cup ripe mango pulp
2 eggs
1 cup sugar

1 cup milk
1 cup heavy cream
1/2 teaspoon vanilla

1. Peel the mango and scrape out the pulp. Mix with 1/4 cup sugar and set aside.

2. In the top part of a double boiler, beat eggs lightly, gradually add 3/4 cup of the sugar.

3. Pour the milk and the cream into a small saucepan. Scald the mixture, remove from heat and add the beaten eggs, a little at a time so as not to curdle.

4. Cook the mixture in the double boiler, over hot water, stirring constantly until it coats a spoon—8-10 minutes. Remove from heat.

5. Stir the mango pulp into the custard in the double boiler. Add the vanilla.

6. If you have an ice cream maker, follow its directions. Otherwise, pour the mixture into a refrigerator freezer tray and freeze to a mush. Remove from refrigerator, spoon the mixture into a bowl and beat to blend well— do not overbeat. Return tray to freezer and leave until ice cream is firm. This should take about 3 hours, depending on your freezer.

189

Kheer
INDIAN RICE PUDDING

As prepared in the Bombay Palace kitchens.

SERVES 6-8.

*4 ounces (115 gm) basmati
  rice
2 quarts (2 liters) milk
1 tablespoon ground
  cardamom*

*4 ounces (115 gm) raisins
2 tablespoons sliced almonds
1/2 cup sugar
dash of rose water (optional)
  (p. 186)*

1. Wash the rice and let soak in clear water for 1/2 hour.

2. Bring the milk to a boil and add the rice. Stir gently until the mixture thickens a bit, then reduce heat. Add the ground cardamom, raisins and sugar, and the rose water, if used. Stir gently a few minutes until the mixture gets thick and creamy. The dessert may be served warm, or else chilled before serving.

Bombay Palace Spiced Tea

SERVES 1.

*1/2 glass tea
1/2 glass milk
2 teaspoons sugar (more or
  less, to taste)*

*2 cardamom pods, crushed
  fine*

1. Make black tea in your favorite way.

2. In a small saucepan put 1/2 glass of tea and 1/2 glass of milk. Add the sugar and the crushed cardamoms, husks and all. Bring to a boil. Strain if desired and pour into a warmed glass.

Coffee Royale

SERVES 1.

1 ounce (30 gm) brandy
1 ounce (30 gm) Kahlùa

hot strong coffee
2 tablespoons whipped cream

Into a heated coffee mug or tall glass put the liqueurs and fill with hot coffee. Stir to mix and top with the whipped cream.

Lassi
COOL YOGHURT DRINK

As prepared in the Bombay Palace kitchens.
    Lassi can be called an "Indian Milk Shake".
    This delicious refresher for hot summer days is made in two styles: sweet or salty. Some like lassi very sweet, some medium-sweet. Our recipe is for a medium-sweet drink.

SERVES 6.

Sweet Lassi

1 pound (1/2 kg) fresh yoghurt, chilled
1 quart iced water (1 liter)

4 ounces sugar (120 gm) or more, to taste
1 tablespoon rose water (p. 186)

Whisk the yoghurt with the milk for 3 minutes, until frothy. Add the other ingredients. Serve in glasses.

Salted Lassi

Omit sugar and substitute 1/2 teaspoon salt.

NOTE: Lassis made in a blender are even frothier and tastier.

Chapter 16

INDIAN FOOD
BEYOND INDIA

People who have eaten a tea room or cafeteria curry have never eaten curry. Unfortunately poor Western cooks have given curries a bad name by making a flour-thick white sauce and sprinkling it with a spoonful of dessicated supermarket "curry powder" (which too often is little more than weakly spiced ground turmeric). The resulting gluey mess has neither flavor nor interest.

By making a light-weight béchamel and adding in a decent amount of a good curry powder—either imported from India or the one mentioned on page 15 of this book—a very pleasantly curried sauce can be made that, among other things, will dress up many vegetables or leftover meats.

To say that this is Indian cooking simplified is to compare the Taj Mahal to a telephone booth. However, busy Americans can make flavor-filled quick-and-easy dishes from the recipes in this chapter. Good cooks will go on to improvise on their own—for example, by adding a bit of good curry powder to a salad dressing, to scrambled eggs, or to add zing to a canned soup.

Chutney Cocktail Dip

This makes an interesting dip for the cocktail hour, good for dipping crisp cooked asparagus or shrimp, or carrot and celery sticks.

MAKES ABOUT 2 CUPS.

1¹/₂ cups mayonnaise
¹/₃ cup mango chutney, Major
   Grey type

3 tablespoons heavy cream

Combine all ingredients, mixing well. If too thick, thin as desired by adding more cream, a spoonful at a time.

Singapore Curry Puffs

These make wonderful appetizers, to be enjoyed at the start of a meal, Oriental or otherwise. They are also marvelous served with cocktails. Either a pastry or a biscuit crust can be used.

MAKES ABOUT 12 SMALL PASTRIES.

Filling:
1 tablespoon (15 gm) butter

Dry Masala:
¹/₂ onion, minced
1 teaspoon red pepper flakes
2 garlic cloves, mashed
1 piece fresh ginger, size of
   almond, minced
10 coriander seeds, ground

¹/₂ teaspoon ground cumin
¹/₂ teaspoon turmeric

Meat:
¹/₂ pound ground beef
2 tablespoons flaked coconut
juice of 1 lime

Dough:
Pastry or biscuit dough to
   make the puffs (see below)

1. In a wok or heavy skillet melt the butter and saute the dry masala until onion becomes golden. Add the meat, stirring until it looses its redness. Add coconut and lime juice and mix well.

2. Roll out the pastry or biscuit dough into a long strip and put a good pinch of the curry mixture every four inches. Cut the dough and fold to enclose the mixture, making either crescents or half triangle rounds. Pinch dough to seal the puffs. Bake in a preheated 450° oven for 15 minutes, or until the pastry is golden.

PASTRY CRUST

MAKES 12-14 CURRY PUFFS.

8 ounces cream cheese (240 gm), room temperature
1/2 pound (240 gm) butter (2 sticks) at room temperature

1/4 cup cream (or half-and-half)
1 teaspoon salt
2 cups flour

1. In a bowl beat the cream cheese and butter until fluffy. Stir in the cream and salt and blend by hand. Gradually stir in the flour, then gather the dough into a ball with as little handling as possible.

2. Wrap dough in waxed paper or plastic and refrigerate for at least 1 hour. Lightly flour a board and roll dough out into a long strip, as thin as possible.

NOTE: This dough can be made a few days ahead and kept refrigerated. It can also be frozen for future use.

BISCUIT CRUST

MAKES 12-14 CURRY PUFFS.

2 cups flour
1 rounded tablespoon baking powder
1/4 teaspoon sugar
dash salt

1/4 pound (120 gm) unsalted butter (1 stick) at room temperature
about 1/3 cup milk or ice water

1. Stir dry ingredients into a bowl. Cut in the butter in small bits, working it into the flour with two knives, until the crumbs are the size of peas.

2. Add milk or ice water, a dribble at a time, stirring with a fork. Use just enough liquid to bind the dough—the less liquid the better.

3. Work the dough into a ball, handling as little as possible. Chill for 1/2 hour. Lightly flour a board and roll out the dough to the thickness of about 1/2 inch (1 1/2 cm).

Curry Mongole Soup

2 cups milk
1 can condensed split pea soup
1/2 can condensed tomato soup
salt and freshly ground pepper
   to taste

2 teaspoons curry powder
1/2 cup heavy cream

Heat the milk and the soups together to the boiling point. Season to taste, adding the curry powder. Just before serving, stir in the heavy cream. Garnish with croutons if desired.

Senegalese Soup

SERVES 4.

2 tablespoons (30 gm) butter
   (1/4 stick)
1 tablespoon curry powder
1 tablespoon flour
2 cups heated ckicken broth
1 cup cooked chicken,
   julienned

2 tablespoons chutney (Major
   Grey type)
2 egg yolks
1/2 cup heavy cream
4 teaspoons minced chives
croutons, optional

1. In a heavy saucepan melt butter and blend in curry powder. Stir and cook a minute to take away the raw taste of the curry, then add the flour to make a roux. Let it bubble gently for 1 minute. Add the hot broth all at once, stir vigorously, and let mixture come to a boil. Reduce heat immediately and add the chicken and chutney. Simmer for 10 minutes to blend flavors.

2. Meanwhile, beat egg yolks in a bowl and add cream, beating well. Set saucepan over low heat, and add 1 spoonful of the hot mixture into the yolks. Stir well then add the yolks into the soup. Bring soup just to boil and serve at once. Top with chives and the croutons.

CROUTONS

4 slices crusty Italian or French   butter to cover the slices
    bread, preferably at least a
    day old

Spread the bread slices thinly with butter. Slice off the crusts. Arrange on a cooky sheet and toast in a 350°F oven until golden brown. Cut into small cubes.

Chutney Salad Dressing

This hearty dressing turns a fresh green salad into a substantial luncheon dish.

MAKES 1 CUP.

$^1/_2$ cup olive oil
3 tablespoons white vinegar
1 tablespoon mango chutney,
    Major Grey type, chopped
1 tablespoon lemon juice
1 teaspoon sugar

$^1/_2$ teaspoon curry powder
$^1/_4$ teaspoon salt
freshly ground pepper to taste
2 tablespoons chopped
    hardboiled egg (optional)

Combine all ingredients and mix well. Shortly before serving, beat well with a fork.

Country Captain

Some say the name of this dish is a corruption of "country capon." More likely, and certainly more romantically, it may be an East India recipe, brought back to England by a British captain of Indian Sepoy troops. Somehow, the dish has become a tradition in our American South, so much so that many Southerners insist it is of local origin. There are many variant recipes; this is one of the best.

SERVES 4.

1 frying chicken, about 3 pounds (1 1/2 kg), cut into 8 pieces
1/4 cup flour
salt and freshly ground pepper
4 tablespoons (60 gm) butter (1/2 stick)
2 onions, diced
1 large green pepper, diced
1 clove garlic, minced
1 tablespoon good curry powder

1/2 teaspoon thyme leaves, crushed
generous grating of nutmeg

1 28-ounce can tomatoes (3/4 kg)
3 tablespoons dried currants
3 tablespoons sliced almonds, toasted in a little butter

1. Prepare the chicken. Set aside.

2. Mix flour, salt and pepper. Rub mixture into chicken pieces.

3. Melt the butter in a wok or heavy skillet over high heat. Add the chicken and brown well on all sides. Remove chicken pieces and add onions, green pepper, garlic, and the spices to the drippings. Stir over low heat, scraping to loosen particles. Add the tomatoes, chopping them coarsely in the pan.

4. Return chicken to the pan, skin side up. Cover and cook slowly until meat is tender—about 20 minutes.

5. Stir the currants into the sauce, and garnish with the toasted almonds. Serve with steamed rice and chutneys.

Quick American Keema

An easy way to turn leftover meat into a delicious dinner.

SERVES 4.

1 1/2 pounds (3/4 kg) of leftover
   lamb, chicken, pork or beef,
   boned
1 tablespoon (15 gm) butter
1 large onion, diced

2 garlic cloves, minced
3 large tomatoes, chopped
1 rounded tablespoon curry
   powder
1 cup yoghurt

1. Trim all fat from the meat and dice fine.

2. In a wok or heavy skillet, melt the butter and saute the onion and garlic until translucent.

3. Add the tomatoes and the curry powder, blending well. Cook over high heat, stirring until the liquid begins to disappear.

4. Stir in diced meat or poultry. The dish is done when it is still moist but no liquid can be seen in the pan. Serve with steamed rice.

Curried Coconut Chicken

SERVES 4.

1 3-pound (1 1/2 kg) chicken,
   skinned and cut into 8 parts
4 tablespoons olive oil
2 onions, chopped

1 good pinch saffron (1/4
   teaspoon crushed annato
   seed may be substituted)
3 tablespoons curry powder
1 fresh coconut, both the meat
   and the liquid

1. Prepare chicken.

2. In a wok or heavy skillet, heat the olive oil. Add the onions, the saffron and curry powder. Add the chicken, and brown nicely on both sides.

3. Crack open the coconut, pour out the juice and set aside while you grate about 1/3 of the coconut meat. Add the coconut to the pot and pour in the juice. Cover and simmer the chicken until tender, about 20 minutes. Serve over steamed rice (p. 150).

Fijian Curry

This way of preparing curry is unique to Hindu cooks living in Fiji, where curry is used to season many native dishes. Fijian curry is more Chinese than Indian, but it is a wonderfully easy and delicious dish to make for a party.

SERVES 4-6.

1 tablespoon (15 gm) butter
2 large onions, chopped
2 garlic cloves, minced
1 well-rounded tablespoon of
  curry powder
juice of half a lime or lemon
1 1/2 pounds (3/4 kg) leftover
  lamb, turkey, chicken or
  beef, diced
1 28-ounce can (3/4 kg)
  tomatoes

1 tablespoon soy sauce
2 cups diced celery, green
  beans, mushrooms,
  zucchini, eggplant, or bean
  sprouts in any combination
  you choose
1 cup stock or white wine
1 can undiluted cream of
  mushroom soup

1. In a wok or heavy skillet, melt the butter and saute the onions and garlic until translucent. Add the curry powder and dribble on the lime juice, stirring a few minutes to take the raw taste out of the spices.

2. Add the meat, tomatoes and their liquid and the soy sauce. Add the vegetables plus enough of the liquid (stock or wine) to make a light gravy.

Gently stir in the mushroom soup, blending well. When the mixture is bubbling, remove from heat.

3. Serve with a large bowl of steamed rice and a selection of chutneys and other garnishes such as chopped peanuts, shredded coconut, minced hard-boiled eggs, chopped onions, crushed bacon, and so forth.

NOTE ON SERVICE:
The festive and correct way to serve this dish is to set the curry pot in the center of the table, and beside it the steaming bowl of rice. A tray adorned with small cups or saucers of different chutneys and sambals is also offered. Each guest ladles a ring of rice and fills the center with as much curry as he wishes, then dresses his plate with as many of the chutneys or sambals as take his fancy.

Sausage and Onion Shortcake Curry

This is a recipe of unknown ancestry but it sounds thoroughly American, and is probably of Southern origin.

The dish combines unlikely ingredients but it is quite delicious. A fresh tart salad makes the meal complete.

SERVES 4.

1 pound (¹/₂ kg) good quality
*   pork sausage meat*
3 onions, thinly sliced
2 tablespoons flour
2 tablespoons curry powder
salt and freshly ground pepper
*   to taste*
pinch of fresh ground nutmeg
2 cups milk

8 sprigs parsley
2 cloves
1 bay leaf
¹/₄ cup white wine
8 hot baking-powder biscuits
*   (see below)*
2 tablespoons chopped parsley
*   or coriander leaves for*
*   garnish*

1. In a wok or heavy skillet, cook the sausage and the onions over low heat for 15 minutes, stirring with a fork to crumble the meat. Pour off excess fat and stir in the flour and the curry powder. Mix well and season with salt, pepper and nutmeg.

2. In a small saucepan, scald the milk, along with the parsley sprigs, the cloves and bay leaf. Strain this flavored hot milk and add to the curry. Place mixture over medium heat. Add the white wine and stir constantly until thickened.

3. On each plate, split 2 biscuits. Cover them with a helping of the sausage curry, garnish with parsley or coriander and serve at once.

SHORTCAKE BISCUITS

MAKES 8 BISCUITS.

1 cup flour
2 teaspoons baking powder
2 teaspoons sugar
¹/₂ teaspoon salt

2 ounces (60 gm) butter (¹/₂
*   stick), or ¹/₄ cup vegetable*
*   shortening*
²/₃ cup milk, approximately

1. Preheat oven to 450°F.

2. In a mixing bowl combine all dry ingredients. With a pastry blender, or using two knives, cut in shortening until mixture is in pea-sized crumbs.

3. Add milk, stirring gently with a fork until mixture forms a stiff dough. Turn out on a lightly floured board and knead gently with floured fingers, about 10 times.

4. Roll or pat out dough ½-inch (1½ cm) thick. Cut out biscuits with floured cutter or use rim of drinking glass. Cut sharply, without twisting. Arrange biscuits on an ungreased baking sheet 1 inch (3 cm) apart. Bake in preheated oven 12 minutes or until golden brown. Time the biscuits so they will be done just as the curry itself is ready to serve.

Stir-Fried Curried Pork

A very easy and authentic Chinese curry.

SERVES 4.

½ pound (¼ kg) boneless
   pork, trimmed of all fat
1 onion, sliced thin
2 tablespoons curry powder
½ cup chicken, beef, or pork
   stock
2 teaspoons cornstarch
2 tablespoons water

1 teaspoon soy sauce
¼ teaspoon sugar
pinch of Five Spice powder
   (obtainable at Chinese food
   stores, or ¼ teaspoon of
   crushed anise seed may be
   substituted)

1. Slice the pork against the grain into very thin slices. Using a dry wok or heavy skillet, cook the onion and curry powder for 2 minutes. Add pork, stir-frying to coat meat with the curry mix—about 3 minutes.

2. Add the stock and cook over medium heat for 5 minutes, stirring occasionally.

3. Meanwhile blend the cornstarch, water, soy sauce, sugar and the Five Spice powder, or anise. Add to meat, cook and stir until thickened and serve at once with steamed long-grain rice.

Stir-Fried Curried Beef

While most fine Chinese restaurants in America include very few curry dishes on their menus, the use of curry is legitimately Chinese, not a Caucasian influence. However, the Chinese use of curry is quite different from the Indian.

SERVES 2.

¹/₂ pound (¹/₄ kg) thin steak, flank or sirloin

Marinade:
1 tablespoon soy sauce
1 tablespoon cornstarch, dissolved in 1 tablespoon water
¹/₂ teaspoon sugar
1 tablespoon oil

1 large onion, minced
2 garlic cloves, minced

4 celery stalks, sliced diagonally into 1¹/₂ × ¹/₄-inch (5 cm × 1 cm) slivers
3 carrots, sliced diagonally into 1¹/₂ × ¹/₄ inch (5 cm × 1 cm) slivers
1 tablespoon curry powder
1 tablespoon soy sauce
1 rounded teaspoon sugar
1 cup water
3 tablespoons oil for stir-frying

1. Slice the meat into three long strips, then crosscut them into ¹/₈-inch (1 cm) slivers. Make the marinade. Put it in a bowl and add the meat. Stir to coat well, and let it sit for at least ¹/₂ hour.

2. Using a very high flame, heat a wok or heavy skillet for several minutes. Add the oil, swirling it around to cover surface of pan. Add the onion and garlic and toss rapidly in the hot fat for about 30 seconds. Add celery, carrots, and curry powder and toss well. Add the soy sauce and sugar and toss. Add the water, toss again, cover, and cook for 5 minutes over medium heat.

4. Drain the meat and put it on top of the vegetables, cover and let steam for about 1¹/₂ minutes. Remove cover, turn heat to high, and toss vigorously for about 30 seconds, until everything is glazed with the sauce. Empty into a heated serving dish.

Serve with steamed long-grain rice.

BÉCHAMEL SAUCE

This is the basic all-purpose white sauce that is as common to Western cooking as garam masala is to Indian. When properly made, as below, béchamel is a useful garnish for many American dishes, and is also the base for several other sauces, such as mornay (add grated gruyère cheese mixed with beaten egg yolk).

This is also the sauce to which poor cooks add a spoonful of U.S. commercial "curry powder" to make a yellow paste served in cafeterias and boarding houses, and which has given the term "curry sauce" a bad name.

MAKES 2 CUPS.

4 tablespoons butter
4 tablespoons flour
3 cups hot (not boiling) milk
6 drops Tabasco sauce

1 teaspoon salt
freshly grated nutmeg to taste
4 tablespoons onion, minced
   (optional)

1. In a saucepan melt the butter over low heat. Stir in the flour gradually, to make a roux. Let the mixture bubble gently 1 minute, until it begins to turn golden (not brown).

2. Remove from heat and add the hot milk all at once, stirring briskly with a wire whisk.

3. Return pan to stove and cook over low heat until thick. Remove from heat, add Tabasco sauce and nutmeg. Blend well and serve warm.

Curried Cabbage, Dutch East Indies

This dish, also known as kool sal au gratin, seems to have passed through France on its way from Indonesia. Nonetheless it is pleasingly unusual and makes a fine vegetable main dish or an accompaniment to a meat dish.

SERVES 4-6.

1 medium cabbage about 4
   pounds (2 kg), cored.

2 cups stock, preferably beef
1/2 onion, grated

1 garlic clove, minced
1 bay leaf
3 cloves, crushed
salt and freshly ground pepper
   to taste
2 cups béchamel sauce (see
   below)

1 tablespoon curry powder
1/2 cup grated gruyère cheese
   (or a mild cheddar)
1/2 cup buttered soft
   breadcrumbs

1. Remove outside leaves from cabbage and discard. Shred the rest fine. Wash and drain cabbage. Set aside.

2. In a wok or large pot combine the beef stock, onion, garlic, bay leaf, cloves, salt and pepper. Add the shredded cabbage and cook until tender, about 10 minutes.

3. While cabbage cooks, make the béchamel sauce and stir in the curry powder. Preheat oven to 400°F.

4. Drain the cabbage and fold into the béchamel. Pour the mixture into a buttered casserole, sprinkle with the grated cheese and top with the buttered crumbs. Bake for 15 minutes, or until top bubbles and turns golden brown.

Curried Tuna

This humble dish is a long way from Indian cooking, but it makes a surprisingly tasty luncheon dish for two. Add sliced endives dressed with a light vinaigrette and a helping of a good Major Grey type chutney, and the meal becomes positively festive.

SERVES 2.

1 can solid-pack tuna (8
   ounces; 240 gm)
1 cup white sauce:
   1 tablespoon flour
   1 tablespoon (15 gm) butter

1 cup milk
freshly gound white pepper
   to taste
1 tablespoon curry powder
2 cups steamed rice

1. Open can of tuna and drain. Set aside.

2. Make the white sauce: Put the flour and butter in a small saucepan over medium heat and stir to make a roux. Add milk and curry powder, stirring until the sauce thickens.

3. Gently stir in the tuna so as not to break up the pieces of fish. Season with pepper to taste. When sauce is bubbling, serve the curried tuna over steamed rice. Serve with a side dish of chutney.

Glossary of Indian Terms

Achar—Pickle
Adrak—Ginger root
Ajwain—Carom seeds; lovage
Akroot—Walnut
Aloo—Potato (also Alu)
Aloo Ki Tikiya—Potato patties
Amchoor—Flavoring powder made from raw sour mangos
Anannas—Pineapple
Anardana—Pomegranate seeds
Appums—*see* Hoppers
Arbi—Yam
Arhar Dal—Yellow split peas (also Toovar Dal)
Arhar Ki Dal—Pigeon peas (also Toor Dal)
Aru—Peach
Ata—Whole wheat flour
Badam—Almond
Badami—Rich meat dish with almond sauce
Badi Elaichi—Black cardamom pods
Baigan—Eggplant (also Brinjal)
Baigan Ka Bharta—Smoked, mashed eggplant
Bajri—Millet
Bandh Gobhi—Cabbage
Bara Jhinga—Lobster
Bari Bhed Ka Gosht—Mutton
Basmati—Fragrant and expensive long grain rice
Batakh—Duck
Batata—Potato (also Aloo)
Besan—Chick-pea flour (gram flour in British usage)

Bhara—Stuffed
Bharta—A vegetable preparation of roasted vegetables, mashed
Bhatura—Deep fried bread made with white flour
Bhindi—Okra
Bhoona—Special Indian cooking technique that combines braising with sauteing; "dry" cooking (also Bhuna)
Bhujia—Vegetable fritter, a form of pakora
Biryani—Rice dish layered with curried meat, cooked together; an elaborate pilaf
Bombil—Bombay duck; small sun-dried fish used as a garnish
Boondi Ka Dahi—Yoghurt dish with tiny chick-pea dumplings
Boti Kabab—Cubes of marinated meat grilled on a skewer
Brinjal—Eggplant (also Baigan)
Burfi—Fudgelike milk sweet with nuts
Burra Nimbu—Lemon
Chah—Tea
Chana—Chick-pea
Chana Dal—Chick-peas, hulled and split
Channa—Fresh cheese similar to cottage cheese (*see* Paneer)
Channia—Coriander (Chinese parsley; cilantro) (also Dhania)
Chapati—Griddle-fried whole wheat bread
Chat—Spiced vegetable dish, served cold
Chatni—Chutney
Chawal—Rice

Chawal Ka Atta—Rice flour

Cheeni—Sugar

Chiroti—Small cakes cooked in deep fat; eaten as snacks

Chole—Whole chick-peas cooked Indian-style

Choti Elaichi—Green cardamom pod

Choti Rajma—Pink bean

Chudva—Mixture of nuts, fried puffed rice, lentils, spices

Chukandar—Red beet

Dahi—Yoghurt

Dal—Any of over fifty varieties of lentils (also Dhal)

Dalchini—Cinnamon

Danshak—Parsi dish of meat and vegetables (also Dhan Sak)

Deghi Mirch—Paprika

Dhania—Fresh coriander (Chinese parsley; cilantro) (also Channia)

Dhania Ke Beej—Coriander seeds

Dhan Sak—Parsi dish of meat and vegetables (also Danshak)

Dhoti Rajma—Pink beans

Doodh—Milk

Do Piaza—Literally, two onions; a single dish in which onions are cooked in two different styles

Dosa—Pancake of Southern India, made from rice and lentils (also Dhosa, Dosai)

Dum—Method of cooking; live coals placed on lid of vessel

Dumba—Fan-tailed shrimp

Elaichi—Cardamom

Firni—Rice pudding with almonds (also Phirni)

Foogath—A cooked vegetable dish, containing coconut

Gaay Ka Gosht—Beef

Gajar—Carrot

Gajar Ka Halva—A dessert made with grated carrots and milk

Garam Masala—Mixture of aromatic spices

Ghee—Clarified butter; also a vegetable shortening

Ghol—Buttermilk

Gingelly—Light sesame oil

Gobhi—Cauliflower (also Phool Gobhi)

Gol Mirch—Black peppercorns

Gosht—Meat (also Josh)

Groundnut—Peanut

Gulab Jal—Rose water

Gulab Jamun—Fried milk balls in sugar syrup

Gulab Ka Sat—Rose essence

Haldi—Turmeric

Halva—Heavy sweet made by reducing fruit or vegetables with sugar

Hari Matar—Green peas

Hari Mirch—Green chili pepper

Hing or *Heeng*—Asafetida; dried gum resins which give onionlike flavor

Hoppers—Pancake with coconut milk, from Madras (also Appums)

Idli—South Indian steamed rice cake; a breakfast dish

Imli—Tamarind

Jaffron—Saffron (also Kesar, Zafran)

Jaggery—Unrefined cane sugar

Jaiphul—Nutmeg

Javitri—Mace

Jeera—Cumin (also Jira)

Jhinga—Shrimp or prawn

Jowari—Barley

Kabab—Skewered meat or vegetable balls

Kabuli Chana—Chick-pea

Kaddu—Pumpkin

Kadhai—Indian cooking utensil, round-bottomed, similar to a wok

Kaju—Cashew nut

Kakdi—Cucumber (also Katchumber)

Kala Chana—Small black chick-peas, whole or unhulled

Kala Zeera—Caraway seeds

Kalia—Fish curry

Kali Mirch—Black pepper

Kalojeera—Black cumin seeds

Kalonji—Spice that looks like onion seeds, hence its name

Kari—Tamil word meaning 'sauce'; possible origin of the word 'curry'

Kari Patta—Small green leaf used for flavor; also known as curry leaf

Kas Kas—Poppy seeds

Kathal—Jackfruit

Katoori—Small metal bowls which are placed on thali (food tray)

Kayla—Banana

Kedgeree—A mixture; a dish made of rice and dal (similar to Kitchuri)

Keema—Minced meat (also Kheema)
Kesar—Saffron (also Jaffron; Zafran)
Khane Ka Soda—Baking soda
Kheer—Rice pudding
Kheera—Cucumber
Khoa—Dried milk (also Mawa)
Khoobani—Apricot
Khoya—Milk cooked until it is fudgelike
Kismis—Raisins
Kitchuri—Mixture (similar to, but not same as, Kedgeree)
Kitchuri Unda—Scrambled eggs
Kofta—Minced meat or vegetable ball
Korma—Rich braised curry, usually containing yoghurt
Kulcha—Leavened white-flour bread baked in the tandoor
Kulfi—Indian-style ice cream
Kulmie Darchini—Cinnamon
Laal Mirch—Red chili pepper; cayenne
Lasan—Garlic
Lassi—Refreshing yoghurt drink; can be either sweet or salty
Laung—Clove
Lobhia—Black-eyed peas, whole
Luchi—Deep-fried bread; Bengali equivalent of Poori (which *see*)
Machli—Fish
Makka Ka Atta—Cornstarch
Malai—Heavy cream
Malpura—Dessert pancakes, dressed with almonds, sesame, etc.
Masala—Mixture of spices
Masoor Dal—Pink or salmon lentils, hulled and split
Matar—Peas
Mawa—Dried milk (also Khoa)
Mehti—Fenugreek (also Methi)
Mehti Ka Saag—Fenugreek leaves
Mehti Ke Beej—Fenugreek seeds
Mirch—Pepper (*see* Simla Mirch, Sookhi Mirch)
Moghlai—Muslim word meaning a dish that is rich and spicy (also Mughalai)
Moog Dal—Mung beans, yellow when hulled and split (*see* Mung Ki Dal)
Mulligatawny—Famous spicy Indian soup; from the Tamil word 'milagutannier', meaning 'pepper water'

Mung Ki Dal—Mung beans, small, green when whole, yellow when hulled
Murgh—Chicken
Murgh Masala—Spiced chicken in a thick sauce
Namak—Salt
Nan—Tear-shaped leavened bread baked inside the tandoor (also Naan)
Nargisi—Dish using hard-boiled eggs
Narial—Coconut
Narrangee—Orange
Nimboo—Lemon or lime
Paan—Digestive preparation made with betel leaf
Pachadi—Mixture of yoghurt and vegetables, salty or sweet
Pakora—Vegetable fritter
Palak—Spinach
Panch Phoron—Combination of cumin, black cumin, mustard and fennel
Paneer—Fresh cheese similar to farmer's cheese (*see* Channa)
Pani—Water
Papeeta—Papaya
Pappadum—Cracker-like bread made from lentils
Paratha—Griddle-fried whole wheat bread, flaky with ghee
Parnasa—Basil
Phirni—Rice pudding with almonds (also Firni)
Phool Gobhi—Cauliflower (also Gobhi)
Piaz—Onion
Pihta—Pistachio
Pillaw—*see* Pulao
Pipel—Long pepper
Pomfret—Firm-fleshed fish similar to flounder
Poodina—Mint
Poori—Deep-fried puffy bread made of whole wheat (also Puri)
Pulao—Rice first fried in ghee and mixed with nuts, then cooked in stock; a pilaf (also Pillaw)
Rai—Mustard
Raita—Yoghurt seasoned with minced cucumber or other seasonings
Rajma—Red kidney beans (also Badi Rajma)
Rasaa—Soup

Rasam—Thin hot-spiced soup of South India

Rasgulla—Cottage cheese ball dessert cooked in sugar syrup

Rasomalai—Cottage cheese ball dessert in heavy cream

Rogan Josh (or *Gosht)*—Moghul-style lamb curry

Roti—Bread

Roti Ka Atta—Chapati flour

Saag—Spinach or greens

Safed Zeera—White cumin seeds

Sambal—Relish typical of South India

Sambar Spice—Combination of hot spices with mustard oil

Sambar—South Indian lentil dish

Samosa—Triangular pastry with meat or vegetable filling

Sarsoon—Mustard greens

Saunf—Fennel

Seekh Kabab—Ground meat mixed with spices, skewered and grilled ('seekh' means 'skewer')

Seetul—Allspice

Semaian—Vermicelli

Shalgam—Turnip

Shami Kabab—Ground meat patties, usually stuffed with vegetables and spices

Simla Mirch—Green pepper

Sirka—Vinegar

Sone Ka Varq—Edible gold foil, used for garnishing a festive dish

Sont—Ground ginger

Sooji—Semolina

Sookhi Garee—Dried coconut

Sookhi Mirch—Dry red chili

Sopari—Betel nut

Souf—Aniseed

Tamarind—Tart fruit with sharp citrus flavor

Tamatar—Tomato

Tandoor—Indian clay oven fired to intense heat by charcoal

Tandoori—Indian-style barbecue

Tardka—Seasoned butter used for garnish

Tava—Indian griddle

Tej Patta—Bay leaf

Thal—Metal platter

Thali—Metal dinner dish

Tikka—Cutlet

Til—Sesame seeds

Toor Dal—Pigeon peas, used in dal dishes (also Arhar Ki Dal)

Toovar Dal—Yellow split peas (also Arhar)

Udrak—Green ginger

Unda—Egg

Urad Dal—Black gram bean; when hulled and split, ivory in color

Usli Ghee—Clarified butter

Vark—Edible thin sheet of silver foil, used as a festive garnish

Vindaloo—Very hot curry originally from Goa

Yakhni—Broth used for cooking rice

Zafran—Saffron (also Kesar, Jaffron)

Index

211